Paul Kegan

Dorothy

A Country Story, in Elegiac Verse, with a preface

Paul Kegan

Dorothy
A Country Story, in Elegiac Verse, with a preface

ISBN/EAN: 9783744662246

Printed in Europe, USA, Canada, Australia, Japan

Cover: Foto ©Thomas Meinert / pixelio.de

More available books at **www.hansebooks.com**

D O R O T H Y

A COUNTRY STORY

𝔍𝔫 𝔈𝔩𝔢𝔤𝔦𝔞𝔠 𝔙𝔢𝔯𝔰𝔢

WITH A PREFACE

[Manby, Arthur]   ⌐

'*Une servante Anglaise, qui a le calus du scrobage aux
genoux*'—Les Misérables

'*Besides, our hands are hard*'—As You Like It

LONDON
C. KEGAN PAUL & CO., 1 PATERNOSTER SQUARE
1880

PREFACE.

A PATERNAL LEGISLATURE, ever anxious, in its sentimental way, to keep women cribbed and coddled and ranked with children, has decreed that all female pit-workers shall leave their work at two o'clock on Saturday afternoons; thus spoiling the task of the male workers (as these have often told me), and driving them, three hours earlier than usual, into the public-house. And so it happened on a Saturday afternoon, in the spring of 1879, that in walking through a certain pit-village I overtook Jemima Derricott, returning from her labour.

Jemima is a stout solid lass of nineteen : strong and hearty, by reason of her work ; grave and earnest, as most pit-girls are. She had on her working dress: her sacking skirt, which had once been a potato-sack, and still bore in large red letters the name of its original owner ; below it, her gaiters and her mighty boots ; and above her ample waist, the cotton frock she wore was nearly hidden by a warm red shawl of coarse woollen ; whilst on her head, tilted upward like the tail of a fantail pigeon, stood her picturesque lilac hood-bonnet : the one apt and

beautiful garment which working women all over rural England still have
sense enough to retain.　And under this bonnet Jemima's broad honest
face appeared : a fresh and youthful face, which at that moment might
be described heraldically as *chequy, gules and sable.*　She was not alone,
our Jemima : she had with her two other girls—creatures of a very
different type.　They were factory-girls or sempstresses, and had been
'playing' all day—for they wore their Sunday dress : their ugly hats,
their tawdry ribbons and sham flowers, their ill-made impudent frocks ;
limp and white-faced weaklings, they were; potential mothers of disease.
One could hardly have had a greater contrast to Jemima ; and as it
turned out, the three comrades were talking of that very contrast : or
rather, the two limp ones were complaining of their work, and of its
effects in some way or other upon their thin and feeble hands.

'Work?' said the pit-girl, as I came up unobserved behind her—
'work?' cried she, scornfully ; 'why, you should work as I do—and
then your hands 'ud be as black and hard as mine is !'　So saying, she
proudly held forth, palm upwards, her large sinewy right hand ; which
was as black as the coal it works in, and almost as hard.　Was she
ashamed of this hand, when she found that I was at her elbow—when I
looked down at it and smiled?　Not she !　She had too much sense :
and as for me, the incident reminded me so of my Dorothy and some of
her mates, that I at once resolved to put Jemima into print, and in this
very Preface.

For it is wonderful, how Nature and Fact are ignored by Literature
and by Art, in this matter of black faces and hard hands.　It is assumed,
in the Fool's Paradise of novels and pictures, that such things do not

exist at all, at least among women : or that, if they do, we must expect them only among women who are ugly and old. Did you ever hear of a heroine with a sooty face or horny hands? Sir Thomas Overbury, indeed, says of his *Faire.and Happy Milke-Maid*, that she makes her hand hard with labour, and her heart soft with pittie : but then she was no heroine ; and what he says of her is as rare as it is beautiful. No— even if the First Chapter displays Griselda in a hovel or in the depths of a mine, you are always made to understand or to suppose that she differs from her fellows, at least in these two particulars. There can be no doubt that Molly Seagrim's handsome face was dirty, and that her hands were hard : but Fielding never says so ; he dared not. Smollett —does *he* ever say so, of any fair maiden? As for Richardson, we know what a very superior young person *Pamela* was : humble as she thought herself, I do not recollect that she ever even scrubbed a floor. Miss Austen has little to do with the working classes ; and even Sir Walter, in all his Gorgeous Gallery of Gallant Inventions, does not, I think, once present us with a peasant girl who is both beautiful and hard-handed.

Nay more : it is taken for granted by all writers that a heroine of the lower ranks *must* be different from her mates, if she is to win the love of the fated Fairy Prince. Even Scott countenances this assumption. *Effie Deans* is first a barefooted herd-girl, and then a tradesman's servant ; yet the smallness and delicacy of her hands are specially mentioned : without such hands, Gentleman Geordie would never have fallen in love with her ! 'Tis the same, I need not say, among the mighty crowd of recent novelists. Their rustic heroines, when they have any, are all of the Dresden China kind: they dance along from village to village, like the sham peasants before Catherine Slayczar ; they wear indeed a country dress, but it is beautifully made, and worn with highbred grace ; indoors, they never do anything harder than dusting, and with a featherbrush ; and a little haymaking is their heaviest work out of doors. And the Honourable Tom Noddy, descending with his eyeglass upon such an heroine, observes at once how greatly she differs from the common peasant girls around : with rapture, he beholds her delicate form, her hands, ungloved, alas ! but dainty as his own ; and · carries her off (in Volume Two) to assume her proper place and be a lady.

Even the exceptions to this style only prove the rule. For instance, there is a clever satirical novel, with a title taken from Rabelais, where a highborn enthusiast resolves to wed the daughter of a cottager ; and it is shown how ignorant, how silly, how unworthy of him, she is. Yet even of such a girl, brought in for such a purpose, it is carefully stated that her hands, though red, were shapely and small. And there is another novel, a sort of converse of this one, and written by a clever woman, who herself (I believe) has risen from the ranks. Its heroine is a lady who has determined to become, and does for a time become, a peasant. *Her* hands are said to have grown brown and hard with out-door work ; and she was proud of them. But then she had a theory to maintain ; and she thought her lover was a working-man. After she found he was a gentleman, we discover that she forsook her theory and its results, and became a lady again. I have not forgotten an author who is perhaps the most dauntless of living story-tellers. His *Christie*

Johnstone and his *Jael Dence* are happy approximations to truth : still —
but I forbear ; it is dangerous to criticise Mr. Charles Reade. Nor have
I forgotten a very fair novel—I forget its name—in which an humble
heroine, who has been busy at house-work, allows her lover to see her
(because she can't help it) with a smutted face. But that was a slight
and casual stain : and she, aghast at the *contretemps*, washes her face
immediately, and returns in ravishing beauty.

Upon the whole, it appears to be an accepted rule of fiction, that if
a woman has red arms or coarse hands, she is old, ugly, and probably
wicked : she merely exists as a foil to the exquisite niece or daughter or
mistress, whose happiness she with fiendish malevolence persists in
thwarting. It is the same, so far as I have observed, in French novels ;
and, to a great extent, in German. Only, as the Germans are a homely
people and their women are mostly coarser and clumsier than ours, you
do now and then find a nice girl who is allowed to be natural and have
ruddy arms or (like the Vulture-Maiden) hard coarse hands. I say
natural : for any one who uses his eyes can see, whatever country he is
in, that the soft-handed white-armed women are not in a majority,
whether of numbers or of merit, even among the young. No one that I
know of, however, has recognised this fact in words—unless it be Mr.
Carlyle and the late Mr. Roebuck. 'Venerable to me is the hard hand,'
says the prophet ; though indeed he is speaking rather of men than of
women. And Mr. Roebuck, advising young working-men as to the
choice of a wife, said once with courageous candour, ' But above all
things, let her have *red arms !* '

So much for prose. Of poetry, there is little to say herein :

because poetry is concerned with beauty as well as with truth ; and the charm

> Of blacken'd faces and of horny hands

fails to draw her ; seeing that these things are perhaps not beautiful. Peasant poets, as might be expected, are specially apt to give small and delicate hands to their sweethearts : and reason good, even if the delicacy and the smallness be only relative ; for his sweetheart represents to a peasant poet those finer external aspects of women which poets of a higher class see in all their equals.

Shakespeare, who spake of most things, has nowhere (I think) dwelt upon this subject. He tells us indeed of the 'pretty chapped hands' of Jane Smile the milkmaid : but he says nothing about Audrey's hands, though we may be sure they were both coarse and brown ; and when he describes 'the kitchen-wench—all grease,' he refrains from adding this touch of horror to her ugliness. He does, however, make Rosalind say of Phœbe—

> I saw her hand ; she has a leathern hand,
> A freestone-colour'd hand ; I verily did think
> That her old gloves were on, but 'twas her hands ;
> She has a huswife's hand ; but that's no matter.

No matter, indeed ! Why, it represents the ὕβρις πεπαιδευμένη of a lady like Rosalind, looking on the hard-working hands of a country girl like Phœbe, and despising her. And this, of course, is what Shakespeare meant ; but I suspect (though I say it with bated breath) that he did not realise the pathetic contrast between a sweet young face and a pair of work-worn hands. Yet Anne Hathaway must have had 'a huswife's hand' when he married her. Wordsworth, whose rustic women and girls are so many, was concerned rather with their moral character and atmosphere than with their physical frame ; and those who have not a special object in writing, may well respect the limits of description imposed by his example—which is the highest of all examples.

It remains, then, to speak of Painting. Painting has come down from theology to court circles, and from court circles to common life ; but she retains the traditions of her origin, and seldom tolerates a servant-maid or a field hand, unless by way of contrast to something better. Dutch *genre* pictures are an exception ; but the aspect of their female characters is so universally common-place or disgusting that it seems only to confirm the polite theory above mentioned, about the wickedness of all red-armed women. Take, for instance, the pig-feeding wench in Rubens's picture of the Prodigal Son. *Her* arms and hands are red and clumsy enough ; but then, she herself is detestable.

The peasant girls in French and German pictures of recent date are, in this matter of hands, far more truthful than ours ; I can only recall one living English painter—Mr. R. W. Macbeth—who has accurately shown the beauty and stateliness which may belong to a coarse-handed English country girl. Of *un*truthfulness, the examples are innumerable. I will mention just one. Some years ago, I saw at the Royal Academy in London a picture of the interview between Faust and Margaret in the garden. The moment represented was that in which he kisses her hand, and she exclaims—

> Wie könnt Ihr sie nur küssen ?
> Sie ist so garstig, ist so rauh !

Now, making every allowance for undue depreciation of herself, we cannot suppose that an artless straightforward girl like Margaret would say
that her hands were *garstig* and *rauh* if they were not so. Yet the
painter had given her hands as dainty and white as a lady's : and his
picture was hung on the line—the place of honour.

Perhaps it may be said that coarseness, especially in Woman, is beneath the notice of true Art, and that brawny strength can never be a
feminine charm.

Well—I deny that any woman (or man either) is beneath the notice
of true Art : and if he or she is to be noticed at all, why then, an
accurate notice is desirable. And as to the other point : I have known
many a strong lass whose strength was a part of her charms, if only by
its very contrast to her other charms. And I refer (though with extreme
diffidence, knowing how slight a hold the Bible has on modern life) to
a statement of King Lemuel, concerning that Virtuous Woman whose
price is far above rubies. 'She girdeth her loins with strength,' says he ;
'and strengtheneth her arms.' King Lemuel, apparently, would not
agree with Monsieur Comte.

And now at length, to come to our Dorothy and such as she : if
you condescend to make their acquaintance. Nothing that Dorothy
is or does but has been taken from life—from English life. Dorothy
herself is mainly taken from life. Her daughter is at this moment in
my service : so that when the narrator of the story says that it all
happened 'only a twelvemonth ago,' you are to understand that, *pro hâc
vice* at least, he is not speaking *now*. This same daughter, waiting at

table once in a farmhouse parlour, took up a large tray, containing the whole of the tea-equipage for half a dozen people, *with one hand*, and so carried it off, not knowing that she had done anything remarkable. But one of the guests exclaimed: 'Well, you *are* strong! You remind me of a girl that was servant at White Rose Farm; and there was a · table in the house that nobody could lift but her, and *she* could carry it easy.' 'Well, sir,' said Dorothy's daughter, smiling, 'and she was my mother!' Many another thing there is of Dorothy's doing, *quod versu dicere non est*; and so I have omitted them. For instance, she thought nothing of carrying a full sack of corn or of potatoes across the farm-yard: and every week in the season, she drove her master's cart to market at the town, five miles off. She harnessed the horse and put him in; she drove alone all the way, with a calf, or a bevy of fowls, or both, in the cart; and when she reached the town, she had no help from ostler or any man; she unharnessed her horse, and put him up in the stable of the inn, and fed him; and then she went and stood in the market, with her calf and fowls, and waited till she had sold them and got the money, and then drove home again, still alone: for Robin had not yet declared himself.

Then, too, her hands—the hard hands of a beautiful girl—are such as I have seen and felt. Her work is all of it work that is done, or that has been done, by hundreds of such girls.

Nor can anyone say it is now unusual, except in the one article of ploughing. You may have seen girls ploughing, in Germany, in Switzer-land, or elsewhere; but not in England? Well, I have myself known or seen at least six English girls who could plough and did plough : two in

Devonshire, two in Yorkshire, one in Gloucestershire, and one in Cheshire. The Devonshire girls were sisters ; daughters of a small farmer who had no sons. They and their father together did the whole work of the farm ; and both he and they were proud, not only of their ploughmanship, but of their skill in all other such labour. The two Yorkshire girls were farm-servants, in different parts of the North Riding. Both were excellent ploughwomen : one of them (she was a lively lass, and fond of a *spree*) on a certain day when her master's landlord had come to visit the farm, assumed her brother's clothes and went out with her team, on purpose that the Squire might see her at plough and take her for a man. He did, and so admired the youth's ploughing that he called him off and gave him half-a-crown : which Mary, touching her cap, received into a plough-man's hand, and strode back to her work, rejoicing in the success of that disguise. Had she appeared as a woman, however, she might have earned more ; for I remember a farmer's wife in Cheshire, who told me with pride that when she was young, and was ploughing near the road-side, the old Squire was so pleased with her performance that he at once gave her a sovereign. About the Gloucestershire girl, I know nothing : I merely saw her driving the plough, as we passed by in the train. But of the Cheshire lass, I have heard many a tale concerning her prowess from her father, a respectable farmer and breeder of horses. He told me she could plough as straight and well as any man he ever saw, and spoke with fatherly pride of the great help she gave him, in that and many other such ways. As for more feminine work, she took the first prize of the county for butter, five years running, and *eleven* years running for cheese. This heroine is now a farmer's wife ; and as her husband has another business elsewhere, she manages the farm entirely, without his aid.

Thus far, I have given only first-hand evidence ·in favour of our Dorothy : I have not referred to that which may be found in the Reports of the Agricultural Commissions. I will, however, quote one passage relating to Dorothy's own neighbourhood, from a report 'drawn up for the consideration of the Board of Agriculture' about eighty years ago. 'It is painful,' says the inspector (he came from Scotland, and perhaps with a bee in his bonnet)—'it is painful to one, who has in his composition the smallest spark of knight-errantry, to behold the beautiful servant-maids of this county toiling in the severe labours of the field. They drive the harrows, or the ploughs, [even] when they are drawn by three or four horses ; nay, it is not uncommon to see, sweating at the dung-cart, a girl, whose elegant features and delicate nicely proportioned limbs seemingly but ill accord with such rough employment.' The servant-maids of that county—and of some other counties—are still more or less beautiful ; they still drive the harrow and help at the dung-cart, even if they have mostly ceased to plough ; and our romantic inspector might be pleased to find that they have not inherited from their mothers those delicate limbs, in spite of which the lasses worked so well in his day. Delicate or not, 'The females who work in the fields are generally the best attired and most healthy of the population' : so said one of the highest of agricultural authorities, referring to that same county and its borders, in 1843 ; and his word is good to the present hour.

The reader (if I have any readers) will observe in our Dorothy's history that suggestions of place and period are hardly ever made.

a

Nevertheless, her story is not without some touches of 'local colour,' obvious enough to those who may care for such an humble and coarse-handed creature as she is. Whom I might now leave, with all her defects, to the candid critic ; congratulating him upon the ease with which the matter and manner of this book will lend itself to ridicule.

But, as I have written in *Elegiacs*, it is well, perhaps, to add a few words about that. We are not ignorant, brethren, of what has been said and done concerning English Hexameters ; from the days of Hobbinol, and Abraham Fraunce, and Philip Sidney, down to those of Whewell, and Clough, and Longfellow, and Kingsley, and Matthew Arnold, and that *lumen purpureum*, Mr. A. C. Swinburne. As for Elegiacs, there was one who said that—

> In the Hexameter rises the fountain's silvery column,
> In the Pentameter aye falling in melody back :

but few have taken kindly to these measures ; their friends are feeble, like myself ; and their enemies are mighty, and rage horribly ; and if they rage against the Hexameter, how much more against the rarer and more difficult Pentameter ? Nevertheless, we, having chosen our measure for no inadequate reasons, have done our best not to break the rules thereof—that one postulate of *accent instead of quantity* being granted : believing, that the metres of Theocritus and Virgil need not be degraded, though the heroine of our Idyllium be nothing better than poor Dorothy Crump.

October, 1880.

In England, by the quiet streams of Yore,
   Is that lone house they live in and they love :
   An upland shaw defends it from above,
With hazels and with hawthorn-clumps, the store
And brooding-place of birds ; and evermore
   Across the meads, the various milk and gold
   Of buttercups and daisies, they behold
The woods and hills, the ruins high and hoar,
   And that old church, to some at least still dear,
   Where the meek dead are garner'd year by year
From love and work, from sorrow and from joy.
Ah, what sweet memories may their souls employ,
   While in a summer eve they sit and hear
   The distant dying waters, falling at the weir !

DOROTHY.

BOOK I.

DOROTHY goes with her pails to the ancient well in the courtyard
    Daily at grey of morn, daily ere twilight at eve ;
Often and often again she winds at the mighty old windlass,
    Still with her strong red arms landing the bucket aright :
Then, her beechen yoke press'd down on her broad square shoulders,
    Stately, erect, like a queen, she with her burden returns :
She with her burden returns to the fields that she loves, to the cattle
    Lowing beside the troughs, welcoming her and her pails.
Dorothy—who is she ? She is only a servant-of-all-work ;
    Servant at White Rose Farm, under the cliff in the vale :   10
Under the sandstone cliff, where martins build in the springtime,
    Hard by the green level meads, hard by the streams of the Yore.
Oh, what a notable lass is our Dolly, the pride of the dairy !
    Stalwart and tall as a man, strong as a heifer to work :
Built for beauty, indeed, but certainly built for labour—
    Witness her muscular arm, witness the grip of her hand !
It was her hands, do you know, that lost her and won her a sweetheart,
    Here, in the harvest time, only a twelvemonth ago.
Dorothy came to the farm, where her mother was servant before her,
    Long, long since—let me see ; yes, it is here she was born :   20

B

Twenty-one years have pass'd, since Betsy, the stout ruddy milkmaid,
 Lay in a garret here, dead, leaving her baby behind.
Great was the scandal it caused ; for many suspected the father :
 Oft had he lodged in the house—made it a bachelor's home ;
Sketching and fishing in spring, and hunting at times in the winter ;
 Visiting, too, when he pleased, all the great neighbours around.
Why should he care for her, for Betsy the rude ruddy milkmaid,
 He, who could have, if he would, ladies in plenty to woo ?
Well—but they said it was he : and the motherly wife of the farmer
 Took poor Betsy's child, rear'd it almost like her own.
Two little daughters she had ; and Dorothy grew up beside them,
 Learning her ABC out of the very same book :
Learning moreover to write, though her clumsy laborious fingers
 Never took kindly to that, hardly could manage a pen.
True, she had marks of her sire—his height, his regular features ;
 Also her golden hair seem'd a reflexion of his :
But with her mother's frame—the strong coarse frame of a farm-wench ;
 Only, refined here and there, shaped by a quality blood :
And, as the years drew on, and she grew from a child to a servant,
 Earning wages at last, heartily working and well,
More of her mother appear'd ; and the delicate traits of the father,
 Save in her handsome face, speedily faded away.

WEAKLY her mistress was, and weakly the two little daughters ;
 But by her master's side Dorothy wrought like a son :
Wrought out of doors on the farm, and labour'd in dairy and kitchen,
 Doing the work of two ; help and support of them all.
Rough were her broad brown hands, and within, ah me ! they were horny :
 Rough were her thick ruddy arms, shapely and round as they were :
Rough too her glowing cheeks ; and her sunburnt face and forehead
 Browner than cairngorm seem'd, set in her amber-bright hair.

Yet 'twas a handsome face ; the beautiful regular features
　　Labour could never spoil, ignorance could not degrade :
And in her clear blue eyes bright gleams of intelligence linger'd ;
　　And on her warm red mouth, Love might have 'lighted and lain.
Never an unkind word nor a rude unseemly expression
　　Came from that soft red mouth ; nor in those sunny blue eyes
Lived there a look that belied the frankness of innocent girlhood—
　　Fearless, because it is pure ; gracious, and gentle, and calm.
Have you not seen such a face, among rural hardworking maidens
　　Born but of peasant stock, free from our Dorothy's shame ?　　　60
Just such faces as hers—a countenance open and artless,
　　Where no knowledge appears, culture, nor vision of grace ;
Yet which an open-air life and simple and strenuous labour
　　Fills with a charm of its own—precious, and warm from the heart?
Hers was full of that charm ; and besides, was something ennobled,
　　Something adorn'd, by thoughts due to a gentle descent :
So that a man should say, if he saw her afield at the milking,
　　Or with her sickle at work reaping the barley or beans,
'There is a strapping wench—a lusty lass of a thousand,
　　'Able to fend for herself, fit for the work of a man !'　　　70
But if he came more near, and she lifted her face to behold him,
　　'Ah,' he would cry, 'what a change ! Surely a *lady* is here !'
Yes—if a lady be one who is gracious and quiet in all things,
　　Thinking no evil at all, helpful wherever she can ;
Then too at White Rose Farm, by the martins' cliff in the valley,
　　There was a lady ; and she was but the servant of all.
True, when she spoke, her speech was the homely speech of the country ;
　　Rough with quaint antique words, picturesque sayings of old :
And, for the things that she said, they were nothing but household phrases—
　　News of the poultry and kine, tidings of village and home ;　　　80
But there was something withal in her musical voice and her manner
　　Gave to such workaday talk touches of higher degree.

So too, abroad and alone, when she saw the sun rise o'er the meadows,
  Or amid golden clouds saw him descending at eve ;
Though no poetic thought, no keen and rapturous insight,
  Troubled her childlike soul, yet she could wonder and gaze ;
Yet she could welcome the morn for its beauty as well as its brightness,
  And, in the evening glow, think—not of supper alone.

STILL, after all, with the life of a rustic maid, of a servant,
  Thought has but little to do ; action alone is her sphere.   90
Action ! And what can she do ? Must I tell you our Dorothy's labours,
  Set her accomplishments down, merely to flatter your pride ;
Merely to let you perceive that she cannot do anything *you* do ;
  Can neither play nor sing ; cannot speak German, nor French ;
Cannot converse—not she—on matters away from her calling ;
  Can't for the life of her tell what your *æsthetics* may mean ;
Cannot at all understand, when you speak about pictures and concerts ;
  Has not the faintest idea either of science or art ;
Nay, is so dreadfully dull, that you all might talk in her presence
  Hours together, and she would not remember a word !   100
Ay, and worse still—for this is a fatal sign, in a woman—
  Has no views about dress ; cares not a bit for the *mode?*
But, if you ask her to tell of the things that belong to the country—
  How cade-lambs are rear'd ; when such a calf should be wean'd ;
How to make butter and cheese, or do this or that in the kitchen ;
  She, in her modest way, simply and aptly replies :
Or, if you ask of the ways of birds and four-footed creatures,
  Robin the keeper himself knows them not better than she.
True (as among the poor and such as live by labour
  Often a skilful hand goes with a faltering tongue ;   110
Or as the knights of old left the tale of their deeds to a minstrel,
  Thinking it scorn to relate what they were proud to achieve)

True—there was much she could do, but could not explain how she did it;
    Spending her skill on the deed, not on the art to describe :
But she could show it in act—could show how to harness a cart-horse,
    How to cut turnips for sheep ; how to feed cattle in stall ;
How you should choose your manure for a cold clay land, or a light one ;
    How you should fatten a pig ; how you should kill him and cure.

'Base barren knowledge,' say you ? But what if it earns her a living ?
    What if it should be her all—all she can ever display ?   120
And I deny it is base : these things must be done, and the doer
    Surely ennobles the work, if she be true to herself ;
Yea, she ennobles her mates : the presence and help of a woman,
    If she be woman indeed, checks yet enlivens a man.
Woman indeed—ah yes ; for factory-girls and pit-girls
    Well may be under control, working in gangs as they do ;
But in our Dorothy's life, herself was her only controller ;
    Master and maid was she, working with men or alone.
Oh—I have yet to complete the list of her many employments :
    First, she can read, as I said ; read in the Bible, I mean—   130
Oft on a Sunday night, when the household meet in the evening,
    Reading aloud by the hearth, taking her turn with the rest :
And, as I said, she can write ; she can fashion her name in a round hand
    Fit for a ploughman to see under his own in the book :
Then, she can sew, right well : for stitching and hemming and darning,
    Whether to make or to mend, none are more clever than she ;
Hard as her fingers are, fine needlework only excepted,
    None in the parish can show stitching more subtle than hers :
Samplers, too ; long ago, she wrought a most beautiful sampler,
    Gay with a cris-cross row, splendid with Adam and Eve ;   140
Framed in her attic, it is, a joy for them that come after :
    Such as her mother made—such as they never make now.

Then, she can scrub, and scour, and swill with the bucket and besom,
 Flinging her pailfuls afar mightily over the yard ;
Sweeping the water away with rapid and vigorous movement,
 Till on the clean wet flags never a footmark appears :
And all over the house you may hear her on Saturdays, always,
 Down on her hands and knees, lustily scrubbing away ;
Scrubbing the warm red bricks of the kitchen floor or the dairy ;
 Scrubbing the oaken boards—parlour and staircase and all.   15
Item—as Touchstone says—she can blacklead grates and fenders ;
 Cleverly lay you a fire, tidily sweep up the hearth ;
Dig and carry the coals ; chop wood, and polish the irons ;
 Blacken her master's boots, and, on a Sunday, her own.
What if her hands for awhile were as black as the boots she was cleaning ?
 They were the better for that—weapons of better defence :
So that, if Robin should come and slyly offer to kiss her,
 'Ere she has wash'd at the sink, 'ere she can rise from the floor,
Up go her dangerous hands, and she cries ' Mr. Robert, behave now !
 Else I shall give you a face black as a tinker's, like mine !'   160

CURIOUS, the ways of these folk of humble and hardy condition :
 Kisses, amongst ourselves, bless me, how much they imply !
Ere you can come to a kiss, you must scale the whole gamut of courtship—
 Introduction first ; pretty attentions and words ;
Tentative looks ; and at length, perhaps the touch of a finger ;
 Then the confession ; and *then* (if she allow it) the kiss.
So that a kiss comes last—'tis the crown and seal of the whole thing ;
 Passion avow'd by you, fondly accepted by her.
But in our Dorothy's class, a kiss only marks the beginning :
 Comes me a light-hearted swain, thinking of nothing at all ;   170
Flings his fustian sleeve round the ample waist of the maiden ;
 Kisses her cheek, and she—laughingly thrusts him away.

Why, 'tis a matter of course ; every good-looking damsel expects it ;
　'Tis but the homage, she feels, paid to her beauty by men :
So that, at *Kiss-in-the-Ring*—an innocent game and a good one—
　Strangers in plenty may kiss : nay, she pursues, in her turn.
Not that our Dorothy did ; though she went to the fair with her mistress :
　She was too grave for that, too unaccustom'd to play ;
But she stood by, with a smile, while the other girls fled from their partners,
　And she approved in her heart, when they were captured and kiss'd.　180
Why did her heart thus approve ?　It was not that she wanted a sweetheart ;
　She never thought of such things—*she*, with her hands full of work !
And, there was no one to have : Mr. Robert was 'meat for her betters ' ;
　He had a house of his own ; and, though he often appear'd,
Mary (for Ann had died), her master's delicate daughter—
　Mary, she thought, was his game : *she* was the sweetheart for him.
True, he had once and again given Dolly a kiss or a fairing ;
　But she thought nothing of that—that was the way of the men :
Haply he did it, she thought, because she belong'd to the Missis—
　Trying his hand on her, waiting for Mary awhile.　190
Then, there was Billy the boy, who help'd her at times with the ladder,
　When she was busy aloft, cleaning the windows upstairs ;
He was too young : he was rude : he would oft run away, and leave her
　High on the ladder alone, just when a cart was at hand !
As for Carter John, whom she help'd in the stable and cowhouse,
　He was a married man, weighted with women and bairns :
So there was no one to have ; not a soul—except Mr. Robert—
　For with the village lads she had but little to do.

THEREFORE, she went on her way, spring, summer, autumn, winter—
　Doing the season's work indoors and out, at the farm ;　200
Caring for little, save that, and the warm and equal affection
　She from a child had known—daughter and servant in one.

Winter—she help'd old John, a-laying down straw for the cattle ;
  Clean'd out the stable and byres, nothing afraid of the bull ;
Help'd at the pig-killing too, and clean'd out the pigstye after ;
  She never thought, not she, *that* was a trouble to do :
Spring—she look'd after the lambs, and the calves that wanted suckling ;
  Work'd in the fields too, a bit, cleaning the land, or at plough.
Well can our Dorothy plough—as a girl, she learnt it and loved it ;
  Leading the teams, at first, follow'd by Master himself ;   210
Then, when she grew to the height and the strength of a muscular woman,
  Grasping the stilts in her pride, driving the mighty machine.
Ah, what a joy for her, at early morn, in the springtime,
  Driving from hedge to hedge furrows as straight as a line !
Seeing the crisp brown earth, like waves at the bow of a vessel,
  Rise, curl over, and fall, under the thrust of the share ;
Orderly falling and still, its edges all creamy and crumbling,
  But, on the sloping side, polish'd and purple as steel ;
Till all the field, she thought, looked bright as the bars of that gridiron
  In the great window at church, over the gentlefolks' pew :   220
And evermore, as she strode, she has cheerful companions behind her ;
  Rooks and the smaller birds, following after her plough ;
And, 'ere the ridges were done, there was gossamer woven above them,
  Gossamer dewy and white, shining like foam on the sea.
Well may she joy in such things, in the freedom of outdoor labour—
  Freeborn lass that she is, fetter'd by Duty alone :
Well may she do—being young, and healthy and hearty and fearless—
  Things that a town-bred girl dared not adventure at all.
For, 'twas not ploughing alone ; but she wrought with the hoe and the harrow,
  Drove the great waggon afield, carted and spread the manure ;   230
Mounted tall Dobbin or Dick, and rode him unharness'd to water,
  Riding, when no one was near, skilfully riding, astride.
Yes—*honi soit*, if you please !   For the damsels of Brittany do it ;
  So do the bonny Welsh girls, out in the vale of Llanrwst ;

DOROTHY.

So, over half the world, does every one, gentle and simple,
  Women as well as the men—maidens and matrons and all.
But in the Summer, again, from haytime till after the harvest,
  Mary was maid of the house : Dorothy, willing and strong,
Willing and strong as she was, could never do all that was wanted ;
  Cleaning and baking must wait—Mary will do what she can :
Dorothy's work is abroad—in the field, on the farm, in the dairy,
  Churning, milking of course, making of curds and of cheese ;
Tending of cattle and swine, and haymaking down in the meadows
  Or up in Breakheart Field ; haymaking she with the rest.

Child's play, you think, making hay ? Why yes, when a dainty young lady
  Tosses a forkful or two, just for a frolic, in fun :
Not when you work all day, from morning far into moonlight,
  Up and down the long rows, raking and forking away ;
Standing at last on the stack, and catching up hay from the waggon—
  That was our Dorothy's work ; ay, and she did it, and well !
Also, when harvest was come, she work'd in the field with her sickle ;
  Wheat, and barley, and beans fell to the sweep of her blade :
She could keep up with the men at reaping, and binding, and stacking ;
  She could keep up with the men ; she could leave laggards behind.
All through the sultry days, in the silent ranks of the reapers,
  Dorothy wrought like a man, keeping her time with the best ;
Earning her harvest wage—for her wages were doubled in harvest ;
  Earning her bacon and bread under the hazels at noon.
Brown grew her handsome face, her bare arms brown as the chestnut ;
  She too, a labourer still, wrought in the sweat of her brow ;
But, with her hair tied up in a handkerchief under her bonnet,
  And with her lilac frock kilted up gaily behind,
She was a pleasure to see ; and there was not a man of her fellows
  Would not have snatch'd, if he dared, Dorothy's hard-working hand.

But they all knew her; they knew, though she chatted and laugh'd like another,
  Neither refused her lips when the cool barrel went round,
Yet she was proud of her work, and kept to herself like a lady—
  Awing a man by her strength, awing him more by her eyes.
Therefore they let her alone—Mr. Robert was never among them—
  And she went free to the field; free and unaided, return'd.   270
But on the last day of all, when the crop was housed, and the stubble
  All over Breakheart Field shone like a faint yellow haze;
When every sheaf was bound, and the Harvest Home was approaching;
  Dorothy came not afield—for she was wanted within.
Mistress and Mary alone could never accomplish the supper—
  Dorothy too must be there, helping to cook and to clean;
Furbishing knives and plates, and dusty old things from the storeroom—
  Crockery seldom used, kept for such banquets as this.

AH, what a time it is, that finishing day of the harvest!
  When the last load comes home, joyously into the yard;   280
Labourers, women and men, all shouting and singing around it—
  Glad that their work is done; scenting the supper at last!
Labourers, women and men, come gathering in to that supper,
  Silent and shy at first, thinking of what there will be,
What there will be to eat—for that is the principal question;
  Drink we are sure there will be—every one knows there is beer.
Master himself sits first, with his wife and daughter beside him;
  Friends—Mr. Robert, perhaps—friends are the next in degree;
Then, Carter John and his spouse, and the shepherd, and Davy the fiddler;
  Then, all the harvest folks, lads and their lasses arow: 290
All expecting awhile the tender delights of the banquet;
  Each one grasping a knife, eager at once to fall to.
But, though the meal is served, and the guests have begun their enjoyment,
  Dorothy never sits down—she is too busy for that:

She is still bustling about, her face on fire with labour,
  Waiting on this one and that, filling their mugs to the brim;
Washing up dishes and plates, or fetching hot things from the oven;
  Active and ready and kind, caring for all but herself.
Often they made her a place, crying 'Dolly, why don't you sit down, lass?'
  Often her mistress call'd 'Dolly, the pudding's a-cold!'   300
So that at last she sat down, on a bench at the foot of the table,
  Emptied her plate and her mug, drank to a health with the rest;
Eating as fast as she could—for she was the last, you remember—
  Thrusting her trencher away jauntily, when she had done!
Ah, poor ignorant girl, how *shall* we attempt to reform her?
  How shall we soften her hands, polish her rough rugged ways?
How can we ever expect *didicisse fideliter artes*,
  So that her father's friends haply may notice his child?
Yes, how indeed! For, as soon as they tired of the δαιτὸς ἐΐσης,
  Dorothy sprang to her feet, lightly jump'd over the bench,   310
Heaved it up under her arm, and another bench under the left arm,
  Swept off the plates in a trice, push'd the big table aside,
Carried off dishes and mugs by armfuls into the back-house,
  Turn'd up her sleeves once more, girded herself to wash up.

E'en when the room was clear'd, and the couples all ranged for the dancing,
  Dorothy did not appear, she was too busy for that:
And, in the scullery there, still washing and rinsing and wiping,
  Who was it found her at last? Why, Mr. Robert himself!
'Dolly lass, what does thee mean—washing up, when the folks are a-playing?
  'Come to the kitchen with me; I must have *thee* for a dance!   320
'How can thee stand like this, with the lads all romping and laughing—
  'Davy—why, hark to him now—scraping his fiddle like mad?'
'Well, Mr. Robert,' said she, 'I've finish'd my work, very nearly;
  'But I must clean myself first—then I will come, by-and-by.

'And it is kind of you, very kind, to want *me* for the dancing;

 'For there's a many, you know, ought to be ax'd afore me.

'What would my Missis say, if you didn't dance first wi' Miss Mary?

 'May be you have, to be sure ; still, you should do it again :

'Then, if you wish it, you know, you'll be certain to light o' me somewheres ;

 'But you must leave me just now, else I shall never get done.' 330

Strangely he smiled, as she spoke, with his hands stuck into his pockets :

 'Well, thou's a hard-working wench, Dolly, my lass, I declare !

'But thou art something besides : don't thee know, thou art very good-looking?'

 'Nay, Mr. Robert,' says she, 'don't you come joking at me !'

Well, never mind—we shall see, by-and-by, when thou comes to the dancing :

 'If thee don't dance with me soon, George ! but I'll kiss thee again !'

'Fie, Mr. Robert !'—And then she took off her clogs and her apron

 (Not till he'd gone, though), and wash'd ; cool'd her hot face at the pump :

Scrubb'd her rough hands and her arms with the floor brush, as if it was Sunday ;

 Making them redder, indeed, but—for a labourer's—clean : 340

Then she went lightly upstairs, to her own little loft in the attic ;

 Put on a clean cotton frock, brush'd out her bonny bright hair :

Turn'd down her sleeves—for, you know, you ladies wear sleeves in a morning,

 Baring your arms but at night, just for the men to admire ;

But, with these working girls, bare arms are needed for labour ;

 So, when the labour is done, sleeves are a sign of repose :

Sleeves, too, are useful to hide—as Dorothy felt when she wore them—

 Workaday arms like hers, if there were gentlefolks near ;

Gentlefolks do so stare at the rough ruddy skin of a servant—

 Just as if *she* could have arms cover'd and coddled, like theirs ! 350

Not that she knew much of that, for gentlefolks seldom came near her :

 But—Mr. Robert was there ; *he* might object to her arms.

Therefore she turn'd down her sleeves, rejoicing that such was the fashion ;

 Donn'd her white collar and cuffs—oh, what a luxury they !

Oh, what a contrast, too, to the sunburnt neck of the wearer,

 And to her strong red wrists, strengthen'd by holding the plough !

But when she look'd in the glass, there was something, just then, to console her,
  Whether for rough red wrists, or for a throat that was tann'd :
There was a rosy young face, as bright and as brown as a berry ;
  Framed in its pale yellow hair, like a ripe nut in the sheath.   360
And she beheld it, and smiled ; for she thought, after all, for a wonder,
  Brown as it was, he was right : some folks might think she was fair !
Think she was fair ?   Yes, indeed ! she might easily pass for a lady,
  Judged by her features alone : but for her hard-working hands ;
But for her tell-tale hands, so big and so broad—on the outside
  Rough as the bark of a tree, hard as its timber within.
Still, she had gloves, you suppose : at least on occasions of this sort ?
  Gloves ?   How our Dolly would laugh, if she could hear you say that !
Rarely on Sundays at church, and certainly not on a week day,
  Had she worn gloves in her life : why, she had never a pair !   370
Stay—she had one : men's size ; they had once belong'd to her father :
  Gentlemen's gloves : so of course they were too little for *her.*
Gloves ! You might almost as soon see her scented with lavender water ;
  Using a silk parasol ; wearing a muff, or a veil !
And, when that pert little Poll, who likes dressmaking better than service,
  Sewing at White Rose Farm, said to our Dorothy once—
' How can you do with such hands, a nice-looking creature as you are ?
  ' Spoilt like an ostler's with work—how can you let 'em be seen ?'
' *How can I let 'em be seen ?*' says Dorothy, 'how can I help it ?
  ' Me that must work for my bread morning and night, as I do ?   380
' Nobody sees 'em, you know, except master and missis and Mary ;
  ' Well, Mr. Robert, perhaps ; *he* must be used to 'em now.
' But if they did, what o' that ? I'm sure they may see 'em and welcome :
  ' See 'em, and feel if they like ; *then* they'll find out if they're hard !
' Why, when we stand to be hired—farm-wenches, I mean, such as I am—
  ' Up at the Martlemas Fair, don't they look first at our hands ?
' Ay, and the lass 'at has hands showing work as plainly as mine does
  ' *She* gets the Godspenny first—*she* is the one they would choose.

'*Spoilt*, did yóu say? Well, I know I reckon my hands is my fortune :

'*I'm* not ashamed of 'em—no, nor of the work they can do !'   390

Such was her argument still ; she was not ashamed of her calling,

Nor of its outward signs—homely, uncouth, if they were ;

She was contented : '*Because she had never known anything better ?*'

Lucky for her, I should say, not to know anything worse !

And she had known nothing worse than a simple and innocent girlhood,

Spent among rural scenes, country delights and employ :

Under a kindhearted dame, amid cheerful and lowly companions,

Fond of their life, like her ; caring for little beyond.

Regular open-air work, and home-made food in abundance,

Strengthen'd her spirit and frame, straighten'd her lusty young limbs ;   400

So that at length she was fit for her place as a wife and a mother—

Mother of men like herself ; Englishmen, sturdy and tall.

Ah, but whose wife will she be ? That is still but a faraway question,

Since she has never allow'd even a sweetheart, as yet :

And we have left her alone, this long, long while, in her attic,

Her, who could put on her things, bonnet and all, in a trice !

So that in five minutes' time she was down in the spacious old kitchen,

Just with a blush on her cheek, feeling it strange to be thus :

Just with a bright red blush through her brown skin melting and glowing,

Like to a sunrise in spring, mask'd by dun clouds of the dawn.   410

'Here is our Dolly !' cried one ; and 'Dolly's come back !' said another :

So they were pleased, it appear'd, when she came into the room.

Even her mistress spoke ; saying, 'Master shall handsel thee, Dolly !'

'Ay,' said her goodman, 'I will ; Dolly, my girl, come along !'

Ere she could think, they were off ; the strong in the grasp of the stronger :

Down the long dance, and again up to the top, and away !

And at the end, when he turn'd, and kiss'd her cheek for remembrance,

That was an honour indeed ! Missis had noticed it, too :

'Father!' she laughingly said, 'is thou kissing our Dolly before me?'
  'Ay!' cried the cheery old man; 'wife, here's another for thee!'   420
So they all laugh'd, sitting round; and Dolly stood panting beside them,
  Stood with her hands on her hips, taking it easy awhile.
Taking it easy—and yet looking furtively round at the dancers,
  When the next dance began: just to see who might be there;
Who might be dancing with whom—Mr. Robert, no doubt, with Miss Mary;
  Yes—there she was in his arms, looking as pleased as a bride!
Dorothy too was pleased, to see them so happy together—
  Yes, for 'He's doing,' she thought, 'just what I ax'd him to do:'
So, she was pleased, of course; but when Jumping Jack from the village
  Came with a sheepish smile, ask'd her to foot it with him,   430
Somehow, she wish'd in her heart that she had the luck of Miss Mary;
  Born in the regular way, sure to inherit a farm.
Still, she forgot all that, when Jumping Jack, in his wild way,
  Gallop'd all over the floor, keeping her galloping too;
Stamping and ramping about, through the boisterous crowded kitchen;
  Envied, by some for his skill, and for his partner by all.
'Eh, you're a good 'un!' he said; for Dorothy throughly enjoy'd it:
  Quiet and grave as she was, careless of pleasures like this,
Once they had enter'd the dance, she was carried away by excitement;
  Proving herself, here too, strongest and swiftest of all.   440
Yet she was wearied at last: 'Oh, Jack, this is harder than threshing!
  'Pull up, my lad, for a bit—let's get our breath, and sit down:
'Eh, how I'm blown, to be sure! it's fit to try *any* one, this is!
  'Take some one else, now do; Missis 'll want me, I'm sure.'
Thus, with a smile, she prevail'd; and he saunter'd away to another,
  Saying 'I'll clip her again; Dolly's the market for me!'
So said the men, every one, though they couldn't all deal at that market;
  Nay, even women approved—all but a critical few:
Such as the two Misses Smith; but they were a tradesman's daughters;
  She, a farm-servant, indeed! what could they care about *her*?   450

' Look at her moggany face,' said Tabitha Smith to Jemima,
  ' Shining with 'eat, I declare—ay, she is wipin' it now !
' Wipin' 'er face, did ye see, wi' the hend of 'er large white hapron ;
  ' My ! what a hignorant thing—isn't she vulgar, oh no ! '
' Yes,' said Jemima, ' to think of 'er 'avin' a hapron to dance in !
  ' Them sort o' girls never knows *what* a young lady should wear :
' Look at 'er great coarse 'ands—why, a 'edger's gloves wouldn't fit.'em—
  ' Spread on her knees like paws ; sure, she might 'ide 'em, for once ! '
So spake the two Misses Smith ; fastidious, fine-spoken damsels,
  Proudly aware as their Pa baked the best bread for the 'All :   460
Also that pert little Poll, with her dressmaking gewgaws about her,
  Wonder'd how Dolly could bear dressing as plain as she did :
Never a sprig in her hair, nor a bit of a bow on her bosom—
  Only an apron, you know ; only a clean cotton frock !
As for the apron, well—one could overlook that, in a servant ;
  She had her work to do, after the dancing was done :
' But,' said the pert little Poll, ' as her 'ands is so *very* 'ardworking,
  ' She might 'ave 'id 'em, this once ; might ha' wore mittens, at least.'—

Thus while our Dorothy fared with the witty and wise of her own sex,
  She neither heeded nor heard : sitting alone by the wall—   470
Sitting and smiling alone, still fanning herself with her apron,
  Or with her hands on her lap ; resting, enjoying repose.
Not very long, though ; for soon Mr. Robert came silently towards her :
  ' Dolly,' said he with a smile, ' where is thy promise to me ? '
' Nay, Mr. Robert, I'm sure I never said nothing to promise ;
  ' Still, if you want me, I'll come—I'll do the best as I can.'
' Ay, and that's better than best !   Don't you know you're the Queen o' the evening,
  ' None is so clever to dance, none so good-looking, as thee !
' Every one says so, indeed ; why, even the lasses confess it :
  ' Dolly o' White Rose Farm—none but our Dolly 'll do ! '   480

'Oh, Mr. Robert,' cried she, 'how *can* you go talking i' that way?
    'Making such fun o' poor me—you, 'at knows well what I am!
'Me, in a plain cotton frock, and nothing to cover my hands with—
    'Really, you shouldn't talk so; really, you shouldn't indeed!
'Them 'at works hard all day can't think to look well of an evening;
    '*That's* for a lady to do, not for a servant like me:
'If I am strong, well and good—I want it, to work for my living:
    'But, to be beautiful—no! Don't you come speaking o' *that*!'—
Thus while she hurriedly spake, disclaiming with passionate ardour
    Praise that another such girl sure would be proud to receive,   450
And while her large blue eyes shone forth on him, moist as the morning
    When every flower and leaf seems running over with dew;
He too was startled and changed; and 'Dolly,' he said, 'is thee serious?
    'What, does thee think me a brute, joking and gaping at *thee*?
'Nay, it was true, every word! But since thou takes on so about it,
    'Better a million times I had said nothing at all!
'Why should it fret thee, my lass? Is it wrong to be beautiful, think you?
    'Some would give half o' their ears, if one could say it o' *them*!
'And, for thy strength, and that—why, we all of us know thou's a wonder;
    'So, if thou won't be the Queen, thou shalt be champion of all.   500
'Come, wipe thy eyes, and get up! else the Master and Missis 'll notice—
    'Bless me, the dance is half done—come, let's be off and away!'
Dorothy smiled through her tears, as he flung his arm lightly around her—
    'Oh, Mr. Robert,' she said, 'don't you think badly o' me;
'*You* meant it well, Sir, I know; but I hate to be told I'm good-looking:
    'For—it was that, don't you know, ruin'd poor mother, and me!'
Ah, and so *this* was his crime—and she knew of her origin, did she?
    Robin himself knew it well; every one knew it, indeed;
But, that she knew it herself, and felt it so strangely and deeply,
    That was a new thing to him, never suspected before.   510
Who would have thought there could be in the heart of so lowly a maiden
    Such a fine fibre as this—such an extravagant shame?

C

She, a chance-child on a farm !   If her wages and victuals were found her,
   Why should she care for her birth ?   What could she know of disgrace ?
So thought Robin—a man of a calm, unimpressible temper,
   Slow to receive new ideas ; strong as a vice, to retain :
So did he ponder and think, as they whirl'd up and down in the dancing,
   Silent ; and she too was grave, mute with respect and amaze ;
For she kept thinking ' Oh dear, I wish I had not been so silly ;
   ' Surely he's angry wi' me—surely he thinks me a fool ! '
' Dolly's in luck,' said one, ' to ha' got Mr. George for a partner !'
   ' Ay,' said another, ' but see—see, lass, how solemn they are !
' He never smiles, never jumps, never freshens her up to a gallop :
   ' Eh, it was different just now, when she was mated wi' Jack !'
Every one noticed the pair ; so seldom together, so silent ;
   Every one noticed, and spake after his kind and degree :
' Well,' said a girl, ' Robert George had better ha' stuck to Miss Mary ;
   ' Dolly's no fellow for him—why does he take up wi' *her*?'
But, as the dance went on, Mr. Robert grew better and brighter ;
   Stepp'd with a heartier step ; said a few kind civil words ;
Said a few welcome words, so that Dorothy brighten'd up also,
   Moved with a livelier grace, trusted the more to his arm ;
And, when the music ceased, and he kiss'd her cheek for remembrance,
   Oh, how she started and blush'd all through her ruddy brown skin !
Just as you sometimes see, in clear bronze streams of the moorland,
   Gleams of a rosy light caught from the westering sun ;
So did she blush ; and her heart felt happy and light in a moment—
   Yes, all along of a kiss often rejected before !
But it was different now : 'twas the token, now, of remembrance ;
   Friendly remembrance : and that—*that* was the thing she desired.
So, when he said ' I must go—I must say good night to the Missis ;
   ' But I shall drink your health : Dolly, lass, get me some beer—
' Ay, and draw some for thyself, thee must be quite dry wi' the dancing :
   ' Be in the larder, thou knows, just by the stable-yard door :'

So (for 'twas part of her work, to fetch up the beer from the cellar,
    Filling the kegs and the jugs, handing the tankards around)
Even that homely request to her had nothing offensive ;
    Neither seem'd out of its place, e'en in so tender a time.
Nay, she felt flatter'd and pleased ; she flew to the best of the barrels,
    Fill'd the great jug—took it up—froth'd it, in Master's own mug ;   550
And, in a trice, he was there—he was with her—he took it, and thank'd her—
    Drank to her very good health, drank to their meeting again.
' Now then,' he said, ' I am off ! But Dolly, this isn't a parting ;
    ' I shall be back by-and-by—back with Sir Harry, thou knows ;
' And, for the present, my lass, there's one thing I wanted to tell thee :
    ' I never knew what thou was, *never*—so help me—till now ! ' ·

They two were standing alone ; and her stable-lantern beside him
    Lighted her figure and face, leaving his own in the shade :
' Dolly, shake hands !' he exclaim'd ; and his voice was all of a tremble :
    She too, so tall and so strong, quiver'd and shook as he spake :   560
' Dolly, shake hands ! '—She was dazed, she hardly knew what she was doing—
    Blindly she gave him her hand ; firmly he took it and held :
Grasp'd it, and look'd at it oft ; caress'd the rough back, and the fingers
    Crooked and stiffen'd with toil ; gazed on the colourless palm ;
She looking at him the while, and wondering much why he did it ;
    Wondering what he could mean, why he should care for her hands.
For, though she was not ashamed to have hands like these, it was only—
    Only because they were signs, instruments, symbols, of work :
Not for themselves, oh no ! for she knew very well they were ugly ;
    Ugly in gentlefolk's eyes : what did that matter to her ?   570
' Girls 'at has nothing to do may have little white fingers, and welcome ;
    ' What could a soft little hand do for a servant like me ? '
That was her creed ; and she knew Mr. Robert lived much among grand folks ;
    Housekeepers, smart ladies' maids bristling all over with pride :

‘ Yes, he must know very well, even kitchenmaids, up at the Squire’s,
  ‘ Haven’t got hands like mine ; he must be thinking it, now ! ’
Oh then, how startled she was, how she blush’d to the height of her forehead,
  When, with her hand still in his, holding it up to the light,
All of a sudden, he stoop’d, and *kiss’d* it—eagerly kiss’d it—
  Kiss’d that cold grey palm, cooling his lips with the horn !   580
‘ Oh, Mr. Robert ! ’ she cried,* ‘ oh, Sir ! how could you ? how can you ?
  ‘ Kissing a hand like mine—how can you shame yourself so ? ’
‘ Shame myself, Dolly ? ’ said he ; ‘ yes, it shames me a little, to see thee,
  ‘ *Thee*, with such hands as these, just like a labouring man’s !
‘ Man’s, did I say ? Why, these are a many times coarser nor mine are ;
  ‘ Mine are not hard—but see, see, they are brown, though, like thine !
‘ But, I am thirty ; and thee, I know thou art scarce over twenty :
  ‘ Heavens ! what work thou hast done ! oh, what a deal to go through !
‘ Well, they are honest hard hands ; and thou ought to be proud on ’em, Dolly ;
  ‘ Proud on ’em, lass, dost hear ? Don’t let folks make thee ashamed—   590
‘ Don’t be ashamed, not a bit, even if they was laid by a lady’s :
  ‘ Wait till I kiss ’em again ! Dolly, God bless thee—good-bye ! ’

GONE ? He was gone ; and she stood gazing after him out of the doorway,
  All in a trance, as it were ; scarce knowing how she got there !
But when she came to herself, she held up her hand to the lantern,
  Look’d at its hard grey palm, kiss’d it—the very same place—
Kiss’d it, and fray’d her soft lips with the touch of its rough rugged edges ;
  Kiss’d it, and thought, ‘ What a hand, *this*, to have kisses from him ! ’
Ay, and with that came tears ; not of shame for a thing so unsightly,
  No, nor of love—not quite : but of great joy, and of pride :   600
Pride, that she was not despised ; that even a hand such as hers was
  Thus had been kiss’d, and by *him*—by Mr. Robert, you know !

---

       * ‘ Wie kännt Ihr sie nur küssen ?
         Sie ist so garstig, ist so rauh ! ’

Joy, too, great joy, at his words : he had said that she never should mind it,
  Nay, should be proud, he had said, both of her work and her hands ;
And (for in spite of herself, 'twas a thing she was fain to rejoice in)
  Said he was coming back soon ; said, he should do it again !
She had thought thus of her work, but seldom had ventured to speak it ;
  Knowing what others would say—chiefly, that pert little Poll ;
Now, it was true ! he had said : and she held them both up, in her folly,
  Held up her two coarse hands, look'd at them fondly— and sigh'd !   610
Sigh'd—for she thought, after all, they could never be fit to be *his* hands,
  Even if he—and she paused : ' Oh, what a silly am I ! '—

Whether it was—who knows? that her conscience was pricking within her,
  Or 'twas her mistress's voice, hurriedly calling her name ;
Sudden she dropp'd her hands, and rush'd to the pump in the corner ;
  Cool'd her wet eyes and her face, made herself sprightly again ;
Ran to the kitchen door, but open'd it slowly and calmly,
  Making as if it was naught, all that had happen'd just now :
All she had heard and seen, the tumult and whirl of her feelings—
  Making as if was naught : Ah, what a hypocrite, she !   620
' Dolly, where *have* you been ? ' said the Missis, half rising to meet her ;
  ' Master's been calling o' you, wanting the key o' the beer !
' Why, all the folks has just gone, and nobody here to attend 'em !
  ' What was you doing, and why didn't you answer afore ? '—
' I never heard, ma'am, I sure ! I never heard Master a-calling,
  ' I never thought it was time—surely I haven't been long ?
' I've been a-fetching of beer—Mr. Robert, he sent me to draw it—
  ' Said he could do with a glass—told me to get it—and so,
' So, ma'am, I fill'd him the jug—I knew you and Master 'ud wish it ;
  ' Brought it, and waited a bit—just till he'd drunk it and gone.'—   630
Such was her story ; and oh, how many a story of passion
  Wears such a probable face, is so untruthfully true !

Simpletons, not to have seen that her face was redder than ever,
  And that her eyes look'd down while she was telling the tale !
But, as they both knew well she was honest and good, they believed her :
  Only, they thought it strange, he should have kept her so long.
' Beer ?' said her master, ' of course ! you was right to get beer for him, Dolly,
  ' Still, I do wonder, wife, he never ax'd it o' me ! '
' Tut ! never mind,' said the dame : ' get along, get along to your work, girl !
  ' Put out the lights—lock the doors—quick, and be off to your bed !   640
' Things may be left all night ; but mind you're up early to-morrow—
  ' Oh, what a clearing there 'll be ! Oh, what a mess they have made ! '—
Thankfully, Dolly obey'd ; did her work, and ran up to her attic ;
  Lightly undress'd, said her prayers, jump'd into bed, and lay down ;
Lay in her small truckle bed, with the sloping roof just above her ;
  Lay for a moment, and then—then, was asleep, like a child.

'TWAS but a poor little room ; a farm-servant's loft in a garret ;
  One small window and door ; never a chimney at all :
One little stool by the bed, and a remnant of cast-away carpet :
  But on the floor, by the wall, carefully dusted and bright,   650
Stood the green-painted box, our Dorothy's closet and wardrobe,
  Holding her treasures, her all—all that she own'd in the world !
Linen and hosen were there, coarse linen and home-knitted hosen ;
  Handkerchiefs bought at the fair, aprons and smocks not a few ;
Kirtles for warmth when afield, and frocks for winter and summer,
  Blue-spotted, lilac, grey ; cotton and woollen and serge ;
All her simple attire, save the clothes she felt most like herself in—
  Rough coarse workaday clothes, fit for a labourer's wear.
There was her Sunday array—the boots, and the shawl, and the bonnet,
  Solemnly folded apart, not to be lightly assumed :   660
There was her jewelry too ; 'twas a brooch (she had worn it this evening)
  Made of a cairngorm stone—really too splendid for her !

Which on a Martlemas Day Mr. Robert had bought for a fairing :
   Little she thought, just then, how she would value it now !
As for her sewing gear, her housewife, her big brass thimble,
   Knitting and suchlike work, such as her fingers could do,
That was away downstairs, in a dresser-drawer in the kitchen,
   Ready for use of a night, when she was tidied and clean.
Item, up there in the chest were her books ; *The Dairyman's Daughter* :
   Ballads : *The Olney Hymns :* Bible and Prayer-book, of course :   670
That was her library ; these were the limits of Dorothy's reading ;
   Wholesome, but scanty indeed : was it then all that she knew ?
Nay, for like other good girls, she had profited much by her schooling
   Under the mighty three—Nature, and Labour, and Life :
Mightier they than books ; if books could have only come after,
   Thoughts of instructed minds filtering down into hers.
That was impossible now ; what she had been, she was, and she would be ;
   Only a farm-serving lass—only a peasant, I fear !

Well—on that green-lidded box, her name was painted in yellow ;
   Dorothy Crump were the words.   Crump ? what a horrible name !   680
Yes, but they gave it to her, because (like the box) 'twas her mother's ;
   Ready to hand—though of course *she* had no joy in the name :
She had no kin—and indeed, she never had needed a surname ;
   Never had used one at all, never had made one her own :
' Dolly ' she was to herself, and to every one else she was ' Dolly ' ;
   Nothing but ' Dolly ' ; and so, that was enough for a name.
Thus then, her great green box, her one undoubted possession,
   Stood where it was ; like her, ' never went nowhere ' at all ;
Waited, perhaps, as of old some beautiful Florentine bride-chest,
   Till, in the fulness of time, He, the Beloved, appears.—   690
Was there naught else in her room ? nothing handy for washing or dressing ?
   Yes ; on a plain deal stand, bason, and ewer, and dish :

All of them empty, unused ; for the sink was the place of her toilet ;
  Save on a Sunday—and then, she too could dress at her ease :
Then, by the little sidewall of the diamonded dormer-window
  She at a sixpenny glass brush'd out her bonny bright hair.
Ah, what a poor little room ! Would *you* like to sleep in it, ladies ?
  Innocence sleeps there unharm'd ; Honour, and Beauty, and Peace—
Love, too, has come ; and with these, even dungeons were easily cheerful :
  But, for our Dorothy's room, it is no dungeon at all.   700
No ! through the latticed panes of the diamonded dormer-window
  Dorothy looks on a world free and familiar and fair :
Looks on the fair farmyard, where the poultry and cattle she lives with
  Bellow and cackle and low—music delightful to her ;
Looks on the fragrant fields, with cloud-shadows flying above them,
  Singing of birds in the air, woodlands and waters around.
She in those fragrant meads has wrought, every year of her girlhood ;
  Over those purple lands she, too, has follow'd the plough ;
And, like a heifer afield, or a lamb that is yean'd in the meadows,
  She, to herself and to us, seems like a part of it all.   710

WHAT is she dreaming of now ? for the moon is up, and I see her
  Laid in her small truckle bed under the bright-colour'd quilt—
Under the patchwork quilt, all cunningly fitted together,
  Made of her old cotton frocks, made by herself long ago.
Ah, 'tis a dream of to-day, of its arduous joys and its wonders ;
  All that has happen'd, and much—much that is yet for to come !
Do we not know that in dreams we are ever forecasting the future,
  Framing out things that should be, though they may never come true ?
Such was our Dorothy's dream : she sat on her box in a waggon,
  Right through the village, and then up to the Castle itself ;   720
For she had even attain'd to a scull'ry-maid's place at the Squire's—
  Oh, what a rise in the world ! Oh, what an honour, for her !

And with her heart in her mouth, as she enter'd the house by the kitchens,
    Wonderful footmen around titter'd and stared at her ways ;
Just as they really had done, when she, going once with the butter,
    Stood such a while at the door, fearful of all she beheld.
Then, in her dream, she was sent—to be seen, and inspected, and order'd,
    Straight to the housekeeper's room : silent, she stood by the door ;
Curtsey'd, and stood by the door, feeling ever so frighten'd and awkward,
    While Mrs. Jellifer sat giving her awful commands.   730
But, in the morning, it seem'd, when Dolly was cleaning the kitchen,
    Just risen up from her knees, cleaning and working away,
Who should come in at the door but My Lady—My Lady Sophia,
    Mistress of that great House, daughter (they said) to a Lord !
She, who so seldom was here, except at the shooting in autumn,
    She, the great lady herself, came to the kitchen alone !
Oh, how our Dorothy blush'd and curtsey'd and flutter'd and trembled,
    Suddenly thus to be seen by such a Missis as that !
Thus, in her working clothes, with her tell-tale hands, and her bare arms,
    Standing unable to fly, fix'd by that masterful gaze :   740
For with a masterful gaze the Lady Sophia survey'd her,
    Looking (she look'd so in church) stately and cold, like a ghost.
' Girl, who are you ? ' said the Dame ; ' you are not the new scull'ry-maid, surely ?
    ' What, have they let you come here straight from a common farmhouse ?
' Look at your face, and your arms ! and your hands are as coarse as a ploughman's—
    ' *You* are not fit to wash up dishes and plates such as mine :
' Send Mrs. Jellifer here ! '—But, just as the culprit was going,
    Lo, Mr. Robert appear'd ; started, yet was not afraid ;
Was not ashamed of *her*, for, touching his brow to my Lady,
    Sudden he sprang to her side, seized her rough hand, and began—   750
Ah, and what was it he said ? For, alas ! we have lost it for ever :
    E'en at that critical time, e'en at the point of her dream,
Came through the diamonded panes, 'twixt the blind and the window, a sunbeam ;
    Lighted on Dorothy's face, melted her fancies away.

' What was he going to tell ? ' cried Dorothy, starting and waking :
   ' Oh, it was only a dream—why, there's the sun, I declare !
' Missis, she told me last night I must sure to be early this morning—
   ' Eh, if she *should* be up first, won't she be angry wi' me ! '
Lightly she sprang out of bed, and flung on her clothes in a moment ;
   Lightly she ran downstairs, all but forgetting her prayers ;
And by the kitchen clock it was half past five, to a minute :
   So, she was not very late ; nobody else was astir.

THUS then, at half past five, her day was begun, and her labour :
   Opening of windows and doors, cleaning of grates and of hearths ;
Wiping of settles and chairs, and sweeping and swilling and scouring,
   Everywhere over the house, half through a long summer day.
Is it not sad, do you think, to see Dorothy drudging and scouring,
   Scrubbing the dirty floor, where she had danced like a guest ?
Prone on her hands and knees, crawling under the tables and benches,
   She, who was praised overnight, she, who was Queen of the ball ?
Well—not a thought of all this ever enter'd the head of our Dolly :
   Work was her daily delight ; holidays seldom and few ;
And, though she liked them right well, she thought of them, too, as a servant—
   One who must buy with her hands all the brief bliss she enjoy'd,
As she was buying it now : by cleaning and tidying after ;
   Mending what others had marr'd ; setting their chaos to rights.

You, who are fair, who are belles, who glitter all night in your triumph,
   Breakfasting late the next day, tended and dress'd by a maid,
How would you care for a ball, if you had to be up in the morning
   Doing what Dorothy did—ay, and perforce, and for hire ?—
Oh, what a difference it makes, being a lady, or only a woman !
   Dorothy knew it quite well—she was a woman, you know—

She, though she seldom had seen and never had talk'd with a lady,
  She understood it ; and thought—what? *That she wouldn't exchange.*
Thought that she wouldn't exchange her life for the life of a lady ;
  Wouldn't give up what she was, not to be ever so fine !
Ah, poor thing ! you perceive it was ignorance saved her from envy—
  Envy of all we possess, culture and leisure and wealth :
Had she but known of these things, and the joys and the lovers they bring us,
  She would have prick'd up her ears, she would have wish'd for them too !   790
No, I think not ; for you see, she was busy with things that are useful :
  Every-day duties, I mean—such as are always to do.
But there was one thing she wish'd : that she could have been, like Miss Mary,
  Blest with a nice little sum, if she should happen to wed.
Oh, how prosaic ! Of course, you and I never think of such matters :
  We are too cultured for that ; *we* always marry for love :
Love ? Why, 'twas that, and naught else, made her wish for a trumpery fortune,
  Just to outweigh, so she thought, all that was poor in herself ;
So that—whoever he was—the man that should seek her a-wooing,
  Might be contented, perhaps ; might not repent of his choice.   800

AND, it was strange—but to-day, when her cleaning and scrubbing were over,
  When she was tidied and wash'd, ready to go to the farm,
As she went forth with her pails to call up the kine for the milking
  (She was too throng in the morn, Billy had done it instead)
As she came back down the lane, with the meek cows walking before her,
  There was Miss Mary herself ! ' Dolly,' she said, ' is it you ?
' Oh, I'm so glad we're alone ! For there's something I wanted to ax' you—
  ' Something I couldn't, at home—mother is always about.
' Father, he says it was *you* saw him off when he went—Mr. Robert ;
  ' Tell me, now, what did he say ? Did he say where he was gone ?   810
Dolly look'd up ; and she thought—yes, she thought her young Missis was blushing
  Then she look'd down ; and she felt ' I must be honest, and tell—

' *Not* the whole truth—not now—that wouldn't be nice, nor respectful ;

  ' But, just a little at least ; something, at least, that is true.'

' Yes, it was me saw him off ; for he sent me to fetch it, Miss Mary—

  ' Sent me to fetch him the beer, just as he started to go.

' And, when he went, he did say—for of course I should never have ax'd him—

  ' He was to go with the Squire, off with Sir Harry, to shoot.'

' Gone with Sir Harry, he is ? Oh, Dolly, he might ha' told *me*, then !

  ' That wasn't like him, you know ; that wasn't friendly or kind !   820

' Dolly, you're more of a friend, a sister almost, nor a servant ;

  ' Else I could almost think he was a-courting of *you* ! '

' Me, Miss ! ' (she always said *Miss*, though many a farm-servant does not ;

  If she obeys, 'tis enough ; no one expects any more)—

' Me, Miss ! why should he ?   What, *him*, head-gamekeeper up at the Squire's,

  ' *Him* come a-courting a girl hasn't a penny, like me ?

' No—if you want him indeed, Miss Mary, of course you've a right to,

  ' If he can have such as you, why should he humble to *me* ? '

' Want him ? ' said Mary, ' oh no ! I wouldn't be wanting of no man :

  ' They shall come just as they will, them 'at comes courting to me.   830

' Still, I did think—but indeed, when I look at you, Dolly, I don't know—

  ' Yours is a sweet pretty face, better nor mine by a deal :

' Why, if you wasn't so brown and so big, they'd call you a beauty ;

  ' Some folks call you it now—yes, I have heard 'em myself !

' And for hard work and that, you're a many times stronger nor I am ;

  ' I am so weak and so pale—what good am *I* on a farm ? '

' Never you mind about that, Miss Mary !   You needn't do nothing,

  ' You'll have your father's brass ; *you* needn't work like a slave,

' You are a Missis ; and me—well, I'm used to hard work, and I like it ;

  ' I am a servant, and strong ; that's right enough, to be sure !   840

' As for my looks, don't you know I hate to be told o' such nonsense ;

  ' Let me but fend for myself ; sweethearts is nothing to me !

' Still,' cried poor Dolly—' oh dear !   I wish you had never have named him ! ·

  ' How can I tell what he thinks ?   How can I help what he does ?

'But, you was always so kind—more like something else nor a Missis—

'Seems, I am not doing right, not to be telling you all.

'Well then, he *did* just talk a little bit out o' the common,

'When he was going, last night, when he was wishing goodbye——'

'Yes,' said Mary, 'I knew, I *knew* there was something to speak of!

'Tell me, lass, don't be afraid—tell me, and what did he do?'　　　850

'Well, Miss, there's nothing to tell—it seems such a strange thing to talk on—

'Praising such hands as mine—how can one think what he meant?

'Still, he *did* praise 'em, and said'—she dared not say he had kiss'd them—

'Said, they was good hard hands; *he* didn't mind 'em at all!'

'Praising your hands!' said her friend, 'Oh, Dolly, what *can* you be thinking?

'Men like a hand'—and she look'd, fondly perhaps, at her own—

'Men like a hand 'at is white, and little, and soft, in a woman;

'Praising such hands as yours—*that* has no meaning o' love!'

Ruefully, Dolly replied, 'Maybe not; but I thought as he liked 'em;

'So I was pleased, of course; no one had praised 'em afore!　　　860

'But it was silly, I know; an' I *do* wish you hadn't ha' named him.

'Tell me, Miss Mary—now do—wouldn't you like him yourself?'

Here was a question, indeed, for one girl to put to another!

Mary look'd up, with a smile, straight into Dorothy's eyes:

Straight into Dolly's blue eyes that were eager and moist with emotion,

Brimming all over with—yes! Mary perceived it—with love.

She was a commonplace girl, but a kind and a tender, was Mary:

Older than Dorothy, too; older, and wiser by far;

For she had been at a school, had kept up the thread of her learning;

Long after Dolly's broad hands came to be harden'd with work;　　　870

She had been out in the world—her uncle, the prosperous grocer,

Ask'd her sometimes to the town, show'd her its wonderful ways,

Show'd her its smart young men, its giggling, gossiping misses,

Drest in the newest guise fresh from great London itself.

She was a commonplace girl: no tremulous passionate ardours

Troubled her small quiet soul, safe in the shallows of life;

And she was kind : she could love—for a home, perhaps, and a husband—
　　But to give pain to a friend, that was no pleasure to her.
Robin had liked her, she thought—but she wasn't quite sure of it, either ;
　　And she liked him, she thought—still, she was not very sure ;　　　　880
For, not a long while ago, young Roffey, the neighbouring farmer,
　　Seem'd to be thinking of her—p'r'aps he was doing so still !
So, while she thought of all this, her heart grew softer and kinder ;
　　Jealousy, scarcely aroused, sank before Dolly's blue eyes ;
(Dolly, who kept looking down, and wondering why she was silent)
　　And at the last, she said ' Dolly, you love him yourself !
' Yes, I can see you do, by your talk, and the look of your eyes, lass !
　　' *You* are the one he should have—leastways, you wish it, I know !
' Well, I did think it was me, but I don't much care if it isn't :
　　' When he comes back, we'll see ; we shall find out, pretty soon ;　　890
' And, if he does love you, if he really is wanting to have you,
　　' *I'll* never stand i' your way—you shall be happy, for me.'

Happy ?　Our Dorothy felt she was thoroughly happy already :
　　Everything seem'd to be changed—all things were possible now !
Somehow, it all had come out : there was nothing she need be ashamed of :
　　She had no rival to fear : *she* stood in nobody's way !
And she forgot her cows, forgot the big stick that she drove with—
　　Yes, let it drop in the lane ; stopp'd, and with innocent joy
Loudly she clapp'd her hands—and ah, as she smote them together,
　　Who would have guess'd such a sound was but an echo of love ?　　900
' Oh, I am glad ! ' she exclaim'd ; ' oh, Miss Mary, I'm *glad* you don't love him !
　　' Sure, you'd have said, if you did—then you would have him, of course ;
' For, it would be such a thing, for *me* to be proud and presuming,
　　' Coming betwixt you and him, stealing-a sweetheart from *you* ;
' You, 'at has been so kind, it was always a pleasure to serve you !
　　' Now, it'll be som'at more ; now I must *love* you, as well.

' Yet, what a stupid I am ! For how can I tell 'at he likes me ?

' He is the keeper, you know—ever so much above *me*—

' Wouldn't it seem like a shame, if he wanted it ever so badly ?

' P'r'aps it was only his way ; p'r'aps he meant nothing at all ! '   910

' Nonsense, you foolish girl,' said Mary, ' I'm certain he loves you :

' How can he help it, you know ?   *I* should, if I was a man !

' And, as for being what you are, what of that ?   You deserve a good husband—

' Only, I don't understand why he should care for your *hands.*'—

' No, nor me neither ! it's strange—one 'd think he'd be fit to despise 'em ;

' Oh, but you never can tell—men are so bad to make out !

' Still, if he *does* want me, and *you* don't mind it, Miss Mary,

' I shall be—well, never mind ; we mustn't talk of it now.

' Don't you tell Master, please ; and whatever you do, not Missis ;

' That 'd be worst thing of all—that 'd be trouble indeed ! '—   920

' Tell 'em ! ' said Mary, ' oh no !   You may trust me—they never shall know it—

' Not till he tells 'em himself—not till he takes you away ! '—

Thus, then, they stood in the lane, those two, and smiled at each other :

Two bonny girls—for, indeed, Mary was not to say plain :

And you would think, I suppose, that at least in so tender a moment,

After such words had been said, such an endearment begun,

Dolly all glowing with bliss, and Mary with kindly contentment,

Now, you suppose, they would kiss, *now* they would kiss and embrace.

No, not at all ! Such a thing never happens, with girls such as these are :

'Tis for young ladies alone, dainty impressible souls !   930

These are but rustics, you know, and Dorothy only a servant ;

They were not equals, and that made it more difficult still.—

True, I have seen, just once, two pit-girls in corduroy trousers,

Blackfaced muscular girls—feminine too, for all that—

Who in a pause of their work, like horses that wait for a waggon,

Waited for *their* waggon too ; harness'd, for they were the team ;

And, as you see such a horse fling its head o'er the neck of its neighbour,

Playfully biting her ear, only for something to do ;

So, of those two strong girls, the slighter (she wasn't so slight, though)
  Actually flung up her arms—fell on the neck of her mate !   940
Whether it was but fatigue, or whether it really were fondness,
  Strange was the sight to me—curious, and almost unique :
There was this manlike maid, with her head on her fellow's broad shoulder,
  Clasping her, just like a—well, just like a delicate girl !
What did the other one do, who was bigger and taller and stronger ?
  Did she respond ?· Did she say, ' Dearest, how sweet to be thus ? '
Bless you, not she !   She was good, and gentle, I tell you, and loving ;
  I know her well, and I know how she is sorrowing now ; *
But she was grave, like a man ; she hated such infantine petting ;
  Ay, and in worktime an' all—lasses and men looking on !   950
So, with a powerful thrust, with a lion-like shake of her large limbs,
  ' Dang tha', lëan oop, wench !' she cried—those were her terrible words—
' Dang tha', lëan oop !' and with that, she push'd off her tender companion ;
  Who had been fell'd by the blow, but that she also was strong.
Was she offended ?   Oh no ; for up came the loaded waggon—
  Up from the workings it came, laden with coals to the brim ;
And, with an emulous start, with a habit of duty, the lasses
  Sprang to their load, both at once, cheerily dragg'd it away.
'Twas a remarkable case ; I never have seen such another :
  For, among untaught girls—peasants and hardworking maids—   960
If they are shallow and light, they care not for graceful *abandon* ;
  Having no grace of their own, having no feelings, indeed :
And, if they're serious and good, like Mary for instance and Dolly,
  Life too is serious, for them ; they are too grave for display.—
Therefore, those two good girls neither kiss'd nor fondled each other :
  Only stood smiling apart, giving out love with their eyes ;
Till, when the spell was loosed—' My goodness, where is the cattle ?
  ' Where ha' they gone ?   They are lost—Crumple has led 'em astray ! '

---

* For the death of her favourite sister, who was also a collier ; one of the best and handsomest
girls I ever knew.

Dolly, she snatch'd up her stick, and ran with the speed of a hunter
   Up the long sandy lane—not very far, it is true ;   970
For they were quiet and safe, and cropping the grass in the hedgerows,
   Heedless of human joys—thinking them trivial, no doubt !
Dorothy drove them straight home, and penn'd them in fold for the milking ;
   And, as she sat on her stool, leaning her cheek on the cow,
Milking with hard dry hands (and they are the hands for a milkmaid),
   Seeing the warm rich milk foaming and white in the pail,
Hearing her cow's soft breath, and feeling the stillness around her,
   Dorothy also was still'd, both from her joy and her pain :
Dorothy also was soothed—though *she* never thought about soothing—
   After a time like this, such as she never had known.   980

. END OF BOOK I.

BOOK II.

Now was the autumn come, and ploughers went forth to their ploughing;
 After the harvest was done, after the stubble was glean'd ;
Ploughing the cornlands in, and turning up some of the fallows ;
 Getting all ready to sow crops for the incoming year.
Oh, how delightful to see the exquisite sweep of the furrows
 Climbing in regular lines over the side of the hill !
Stretching in beautiful curves, as it seems at a distance, but really
 Straight as the strings of a harp ; ranged in great octaves, like them.
For you shall see, in the sun, all purple and steely and shining,
 Ranges of long bright lines, all of them strictly alike ;
But, at the end of each range, at equal intervals always,
 Comes a great deep bass line, carved like a trench—as it is.
Masterly art, in its way, and noble, the art of the ploughman !
 Well might our Dorothy feel proud of its ' glory and joy ! '
For she was ploughing too ; in the cool sweet air of October
 She too was out with the morn, scoring the slopes of the hill.
Under a hedge by the wood stood her plough, with its yoketree of scarlet—
 Symbol of all good work—waiting till Dolly should come ;
Till she had harness'd the team, and with Billy the boy to attend her,
 Rode on the foremost horse, fresh for her labour of love.
For 'twas a labour of love, whereby she was earning her living :
 What can be better than that, either for woman or man ?
Always to feel that your work is a thing that you know and are fit for,
 Always to love it, and feel ' Yes, I am doing it well ' !
That was what Dorothy felt, though she couldn't have told you her feelings,
 While she strode over the field after her horses, at plough ;

Driving her furrows so straight, and trenching them round at the hedgerows,
  Guiding the stilts with a grasp skilful and strong as a man's.

Thus then, one beautiful day, in the sweet cool air of October,
  High up on Breakheart Field, under the skirts of the wood,   1010
Dolly was ploughing : she wore (why did I not sooner describe it ?)
  Just such a dress as they all—all the farm-servants around :
Only, it seem'd to be hers by a right divine and a fitness—
  Colour and pattern and shape suited so aptly to her.
First, on her well-set head a lilac hood-bonnet of cotton,
  Framing her amberbright hair, shading her neck from the sun ;
Then, on her shoulders a shawl ; a coarse red kerchief of woollen,
  Matching the glow of her cheeks, lighting her berry-brown skin ;
Then came a blue cotton frock—dark blue, and spotted with yellow—
  Sleeved to the elbows alone, leaving her bonny arms bare ;   1020
So that those ruddy brown arms, with the dim dull blue for a background,
  Seem'd not so rough as they were—softer in colour and grain.
All round her ample waist her frock was gather'd and kilted,
  Showing her kirtle, that hung down to the calf of the leg :
Lancashire linsey it was, with bands of various colour
  Striped on a blue-grey ground : sober, and modest, and warm ;
Showing her stout firm legs, made stouter by home-knitted stockings ;
  Ending in strong laced boots, such as a ploughman should wear :
Big solid ironshod boots, that added an inch to her stature :
  Studded with nails underneath, shoed like a horse, at the heels.   1030
After a day at plough, all clotted with earth from the furrows,
  Oh, how unlike were her boots, Rosa Matilda, to yours !

'TWAS in the quiet of noon ; and Dolly, thus clad, thus attended,
  Sat on a green hedge-bank, taking her rest for awhile :

Sat there with Billy the boy, for there they had eaten their dinner—
  Bacon and bread and cold tea—under the shade of the hedge ;
Under the shade of her team, for the tall plough-horses above her
  Also were taking their ease, patiently waiting for her :
When, from the midst of the copse, from the heart of the mellowing woodlands,
  Firing of guns was heard, whirring of terrified birds.
'Gentlefolks !' Dolly exclaim'd, and sprang up at once to her labour ;
  'Billy, lad, straighten the team—maybe they're coming this way !'
And, with a crack of her whip, with a loud 'Gee up !' and a 'Woa, horse !'
  Off they all started—and she lifting and swaying behind.
Scarce had the great plough achieved one furrow and half of another,
  When from the edge of the wood two polish'd strangers appear'd ;
Each with his gun, and equipp'd with shooting-coat, leggings, and all that :
  Gentlemen both, as it seem'd : guests at the Castle, no doubt.
One was an iron-grey man of forty, or even of fifty ;
  Statue-like, soldierly, calm ; but the quick light in his eyes
Spake of a passionate past : the other was twenty years younger ;
  Still but a stripling, and fair ; fair, with a lovely moustache.
'Ah,' cried the elder, 'I see ! This is Breakheart Field, with a vengeance !'
  'Yes, I remember it well ; and there's a footpath, I know,
'Somewhere about, by a farm, to the Ings—the waterside meadows ;
  'There we can meet them, you know ; that's where the luncheon's to be.'—
"'Gad, though, look there !' cried the youth ;—'a woman, by George !—and she's
    ploughing—
  'What, do they train them, out here—women—to follow the plough ?
'Uncle, we'll ask her the way—she's a social phenomenon, surely ;
  'Which you can quote with effect, next time you bring in your Bill !
'P'r'aps she has heard of your *Bill to Regulate Female Employment*—
  ' "Women and children," you know—*won't* she adore you for that !
'Yet, if you look at her now, you'll admit she's a capital ploughman :
  'See how she helps it along—see how she handles her team !'

THUS while they talk'd, standing there, poor Dolly was ever approaching,
   She, with her horses in front headed by Billy the boy :
Ah, she had only escaped from the frying-pan into the fire—
   Here were the quality folks, standing and staring at *her* !
What could she do ? She was trapp'd—she could but go nearer and nearer,
   Red though her face might be ; redder than ever, just now :   1070
Ay, and whatever its faults, her hands were too busy to hide them :
   Well, she must let things alone ; *they'd* never notice her face !
Swiftly she came to her doom—and the younger stranger address'd her
   ('Jove ! she's a beauty,' he thought, ' Fancy a beauty at plough !')
' So you are ploughing, my lass ? Warm work, in such weather as this is ! '
   'Woa, horse ! ' Dolly replied, pulling her best at the rein,
'Woa ! ' And the plough stood still ; and she, as she stood in the furrow,
   Dropp'd him a curtsey, and said, ' Yes, Sir, it *is* very warm.'
' Can you,' the elder began, with a lofty though courteous demeanour—
   'Can you just tell us, my girl, which is the way to the Ings ?'   1080
' Yes, Sir ; ' and lifting her arm, she pointed down into the valley—
   ' Yes, Sir, you go by yon farm, under the cliff in the lane.'
' Thank you,' he said, and walk'd on ; but the other one linger'd behind him :
   Dorothy wonder'd at that—what was he stopping to say ?
She, in the midst of her work—so unfit for her betters to talk to—
   Wish'd they would both go away ; wish'd they had never come near.
' Ah, then, you live at that farm ? Perhaps you're the farmer's daughter ?
   ' Me, Sir ? ' cried Dolly, ' Oh no ! I am the servant, that's all ! '
And, as she said it, she smiled ; little knowing how well it became her ;
   How it condoned in his eyes all that was coarse in her work.   1090
' Are you a servant ? Indeed ! And why do they send you out ploughing ?
   ' *Men* should do that, don't you know ? *You* should be quiet indoors ! '
Dolly could almost have laugh'd, but she knew it would not be respectful ;
   Therefore she gravely replied, ' Well, Sir, I'm used to the fields :
' And there is only me, and Master, and this little lad here :
   ' I should be shamed indeed, not to be able to plough ! '

'Would you? And what is your name? and what is the name of the farm there?'

'White Rose Farm, Sir,' she said ; 'that is the place where I live.'

As for her own poor name, she was silent ; for why should he ask it?

'*White Rose Farm!*' he exclaim'd ; 'oh, what a beautiful name !   1100

'Yes, now I see how it is '—and he smiled in her face as he said it—

'*You* gave its name to the farm ; *you* are the bonny White Rose !

'Well, I shall see you again ! Good-bye—you will not forget me?

'Here is a trifle, you know, just to remember me by.'

And, with the word, he held out a broad piece of glittering silver,

Such as she seldom had seen, never had had for her own.

Had he but look'd in her eyes, he would never have offer'd her money :

Both her blue eyes were aflame, shining like stars in a frost :

'No, sir,' she said, 'not for me—no, thank you, Sir—I have my wages—

'Billy, get on !' And the plough moved in the furrow again ;   1110

She, with a grand disdain, with a muscular heave of her shoulders

Lifting the share to its work, setting it straight in the mould.

He was discomfited ; he, who had had such success among ladies,

Foil'd by an ignorant wench bound to the tail of a plough !

It was distressing, of course ; but with such an antagonist, truly

There was no shame in defeat—triumph itself were disgrace.

'She is a vixen,' he thought, 'but I like her the better for that, though ;

'Jove, how that anger of hers suited her beautiful face !

'She is no common girl ; there must be a story about her :

'I shall find out before long—yes, I will see her again.'   1120

So, he stepp'd lightly away to the stile where his uncle was waiting—

Waiting indignant, and still twirling his grisly moustache.

'Frank,' said the senior, 'I know you are too much addicted to women—

'But I'm ashamed to see *you* stoop to a creature like that !

'Wenches who work in the fields are sure to be reprobates always :

'How much more, do you think, one so depraved as to *plough*?

'And you should know where you are : remember our duty as guests, sir !

'That girl's master, no doubt, farms on the Castle estate ;

' He is a lowborn boor ; and she, lower still, is his servant ;

' How would you like to be seen stopping and speaking to *her* ?   1130

'Ah, when I've carried my Bill—and it's rising in favour already—

We'll put a stop to all this ; we'll have no women a-field ! '—

Frank, that irreverent boy, had the courage to laugh at his uncle :

' Bother your Bill !' he replied—'why, what a purist you are !

' Uncle, I tell you you're wrong ; you do her injustice, believe me ;

' She is no commonplace wench ; *she's* not degraded at all.

' You should have seen how she look'd when I ventured to offer her money !

' Proud ? Why, she rivals in pride Lady Sophia herself !

' And, did you notice her face ? It was sunburnt and rough, as her arms were,

' But it was handsome withal—gentle, expressive, refined.   1140

' Yes '—for he saw the deep scorn in his uncle's countenance rising—

' Yes, sir, I say it's *refined* : *she'll* never better your Bill !'

' Bosh !' growl'd the other, enraged : ' when you've lived half as long, sir, as I have,

' You'll understand that a girl brought up to labour like hers

' *Must* be degraded and coarse : but I see it is useless to argue—

' Don't let me hear this again !' ' No,' said his nephew, 'you shan't !'

Thus they contended in talk ; each far from the truth of the matter :

But, as is usual, the youth trying at least to be just ;

While the grave man of the world, by his own want of sympathy blinded,

Saw but the homely outside ; noted down *that* for his Bill.   1150

Well—and our Dolly herself, what did *she* do ? and what were her feelings ?

Oh, she just stuck to the plough—finish'd the baulk she was on ;

Follow'd her horses again, up and down, up and down, till the evening ;

Chiefly intent on her work, thinking of little, save that.

But, when the day's work was done, when the plough was unyoked by the hedgerow,

When the whole team went home, headed by Billy the boy ;

She, on the hindmost horse, high perch'd, holding on by the halter,

All in her simple heart ponder'd the things she had heard.

She had been brought face to face with men of a rank far above her :
    Forced to converse with them, too, since they were pleased to converse :   1160
Ay, and what wearisome talk, what foolish trumpery questions—
    This was her first great thought—had she been hearing today !
If they were all like *him*, what strange irrational persons
    Quality folks must be ! Yet, she could easily tell,
Both by his voice and words, his dress and his company manners,
    He had come out of a world larger and higher than hers.
That was just it ! He thought that poor folks' ways were beneath him :
    Things that might serve to amuse such as are clever and rich :
Thought he might say what he liked, talk ever such flatulent nonsense,
    When he should stoop to address ignorant people like her.   1170
Such were her thoughts—not her words : oh dear me, no, not her words, ma'am!
    She had no words ; or at least, only an impotent few :
But she could think, and feel ; and her thoughts were somewhat on this wise—
    ' *Me* a White Rose, did he say ? *Me* give a name to the farm ?
' Rubbish ! But happen, he thought I should like to be talk'd to a-that way ;
    ' Happen, 'twas only his fun—making a game, like, o' me !
' Farmer's daughter, indeed ! When he knew very well I'm a servant :
    ' Must have seen it, of course ; everything shows what I am !
' And to be quiet indoors, and never do nothing at field work—
    ' Never make hay, never hoe turnips and taters and wheat—   1180
' Me, 'at can do it as well as a man, I'll awand you, or better,
    ' *Me*, to be shut up indoors—oh, what a fool he must be !
' How I do hate such talk ! Mr. Robert, how different *he* was !
    ' Told me I ought to be proud both o' my work an' my hands ;
' Seem'd to be pleased, and spoke like a sensible man and a kind one—
    ' Not such a guiser as yon—meaning, one canna tell what ! '—
True, she hated his talk : but not for its foolishness only ;
    Something mor deadly than that ruffled her maidenly pride :
For, with his smooth soft words, and the offer he made her of money,
    Memories hotter than hate went like a flash through her brain.

Maybe, she thought, it was *thus* that some one first spoke to her mother—
Flatt'ring her pretty young face, tempting her foully with coin !
That, and not pride, was the thought that drove her indignantly onward ;
That made her hurry away, spurning his money and him :
Not the mere silver ; oh no—she could curtsey and smile at a shilling
Honestly given and meant : shillings were precious, tᴏ̃ *her.*

WELL for a peasant girl who has beauty and worth, like our Dolly,
If she have strength not her own, thus to support her at need !
Even if rashly she think—as Dolly had reason for thinking—
Gentlemen *must* go about seeking poor maids to devour.   1200
She was a poor maid, too : but if he should seek to devour her—
He, with his glamour of words, graceful and glittering ways—
Surely he will not succeed ?   For that which ruin'd the mother
Gave to the daughter a soul keener and stronger than hers :
Love, too, was fast coming in—the added strength of attachment—
Soon Mr. Robert would come ; soon she should see him again !
Thus then she waited and work'd, and thought of the shooting in Scotland :
When would Sir Harry return ?   When would they all be at home ?
Weeks had already gone by, that day when the gentlemen met her,
Since the great Harvest Home, since Mr. Robert had gone ;   1210
Weeks had already gone by : when the housekeeper up at the Castle,
Calling at White Rose Farm, once, on her way to the town,
Mention'd, in affable talk to the Missis, and also to Mary,
That there was news of them all—news of Sir Harry, at last.
' Yes, they are all coming back ; and isn't it strange, Mr. Robert,
Going to be married so soon ?   Leastways, they say as it's him.'
' Married !' the Missis exclaim'd ; but Mary was prudently silent,
Keeping her heart to herself, till the old gossip had gone.
Then, she also exclaim'd :   ' I'll never believe it !   But, mother,
' Don't you tell Dorothy, though ; don't let our Dorothy know !'   1220

'Dolly? Why not?' said the dame; 'what has *she* got to do wi' the keeper?
'Setting her cap at him, eh? Nay, it can never be *that*!'
'Setting her cap? No indeed!' cried Mary; 'but, mother, I'm certain
'He has a fancy for her—he'll marry nobody else.'
'Why then, I thought it was *you* he was making sheep's eyes all along at!'
'Me, mother? No, not he—I wouldn't have him, at least:
'Somebody else shall have *me*'—but ere they were talking in this way,
Dolly, unhappy, had heard what Mrs. Jellifer said:
For in the scullery near, she was sitting and peeling potatoes,
Thinking of nothing at all; happy, no doubt, in her work;   1230
When Mr. Robert his name had flash'd through her ears like the lightning;
Follow'd by thunder, alas! 'Going to be married so soon!'
What did she do? Did she faint, and scream, and go into hysterics?
No, madam! Fainting and salts are not for wenches like her:
She only dropp'd her knife; and the curly potato parings
Roll'd off her quivering knees, settled themselves on the floor,
While she rose up, and went out: to the barn, for she knew it was empty—
Had a good cry, and return'd heavily back to her work.
Nobody named the affair; and all things went on just as usual;
Till, on a washing day, Mary and she were alone,   1240
And she broke out and said, 'Miss Mary, why didn't you tell me?'
'Tell you? tell *what*?' said the girl: 'Why, that he's going to be wed!'
'Wed? Not a bit! Not he! Now, Dorothy, don't you believe it!
'I'll bet a penny it's lies—wait till you see him, and then!
'Yes, it's just like them girls in the housemaids' room at the Castle,
'Wanting to have him theirsels—making up tales, when they *can't*!'
Dorothy shook her head: 'I canna help thinking it's true, Miss;
There's such a many—and then, sure Mrs. Jellifer knows!'

'TWAS on that very same day, while Dorothy, after her milking,
Went along White Rose Lane, driving her cattle a-field,   1250

Whom should she see but him, the youth with the lovely moustaches,
  Sauntering there all alone, smoking his evening cigar !
Leaning, he was, on the gate of the field into which she was going ;
  Gazing, it seem'd, towards the West : what was he studying there ?
Well, there was something to see ; for the sun was setting in glory,
  Glowing through marvellous clouds, molten, suffused, with his light ;
Clouds all rosy above, like the snows of an Alpine sunset,
  But in the heart of their snow thrill'd with a cavernous fire ;
Clouds that were couch'd superb in a blaze of opal and em'rald,
  Haunting the clear cool sky, lucid and lovely and blue.   1260
Yes, he was studying that ; and Dorothy noticed it also :
  How could she help it, you know, walking straight into the West ?
Her heart too was refresh'd by the sight of those wonderful colours,
  Though she had seen them before, many and many a time.
'What, is it you ?' said the youth ; 'the White Rose maid of the farm there !
  ' Ah, you do well to be out now, in an evening like this !
' Is it not beautiful here ?   And do you not often enjoy it,
  ' Strolling abroad in the lanes, after your duties are done ?
' You have been milking, perhaps ?   What clear-eyed beautiful creatures !
  'Why, they have skins, I believe, almost as soft as your own !'   1270
Dolly had curtsey'd and blush'd, when he open'd his lips to address her ;
  Awed by his presence, and yet wishing he hadn't been there ;
Now, she started and stared—what, again ?   Would he never have done, then,
  Talking his nonsense ?   And worse, making such game about *her* ?
Who would have thought, indeed, that gentlefolks *could* be so artful,
  Saying in roundabout words just what they never could mean ?
It was too bad, Dolly thought ; and she solemnly said, ' If you please, Sir,
  Just let me open the gate—let me come through with the cows ! '
' Oh, is it this way you go ?   Let *me* set the gate open for you !
  Gaily he did it, and held ; but the poor ignorant cows,   1280
Seeing a stranger, hung back ; and Dorothy scamper'd around them,
  Calling, and waving her arms, using her stick now and then,

Till they were all in the field : while he, with his critical eyeglass,
    Scann'd her (she felt it), and stood calmly surveying the scene.
'Thank you, Sir,' Dorothy said, turning hastily round to go homeward :
    But he had shut-to the gate ; closed it, and she was inside !
There he stood, leaning without, and smiling, and holding her captive ;
    Smiling persuasive smiles, under his golden moustache !
' I have done something for you—and will you do nothing for me, then ?
    ' You must pay toll, don't you know ?   That is the rule of the road ! '   1290
Toll ! Though the phrase was new, she guess'd what he meant ; and it call'd up,
    Over her bonny brown face, crimson as deep as the sky's :
What, should she stand like a stock, and a stranger gentleman kiss her ?
No ! And she sprang to the gate, meaning to climb it at once :
Gates were a trifle, to her : she would climb it in spite of him, easy,
    And from the topmost bar lightly leap down, and away !
But he relented : ' Oh no ! Not *that*—I would never detain you—
    ' Only a moment's talk—won't you just hear me, for once ? '—
' Hear you, Sir ? ' Dolly replied, as she came through the gate very proudly,
    ' *You* can ha' nothing to say—nothing as *I* understand !   1300
' You are demeaning yourself, Sir, to talk to a servant like I am ;
    ' Let me go home to the farm—I am no fellow for you ! '
' Servant ? ' he said, ' But indeed I do not believe you're a servant ;
    ' You are too pretty for that. Tell me, now, what is your name ? '
' Dolly's my name, Sir,' she said. ' Dolly what ? ' ' Oh, nothing but Dolly !
    ' Why was you axing my name ? ' For, with a flutter of shame,
All her heart took fire at the thought that she had not a father,
    Save such a stranger as this : just such another, perhaps !
All her simple heart went flickering this way and that way,
    Thinking of him that was gone, whom she could love very well—   1310
Thinking of this one here, this gentleman, dainty and clever,
    Whom she could *not* love at all : why was he bothering *her*?
' Give me your hand,' said he, ' and I'll tell you your name without asking ! '
    She, with a sudden disdain, put it behind her at once :

But, in a moment, she thought, ' He'll see I am really a servant,
  ' If I but show him my hand : yes, let him see it, and feel ! '
Therefore, she held out her hand ; and he snatch'd it, poor man ! without looking :
  'Twas but her face that he saw—*that* was the thing he admired ;
That, and her picturesque dress ; and perhaps her arms, just a little ;
  Though even peasants, he thought, might have more delicate arms.   1320
Lightly he took her hand ; intending, doubtless, to press it :
  Meaning at least to bestow some pretty compliment there ;
But, as to one in the dark, who, feeling for silk or for velvet,
  Suddenly grasps unawares rusty old iron instead,
So did it happen to him, thus grasping the hand of our Dolly—
  Rough as old iron, and hard—terribly callous—within.
Singular contrast, this, these two hands mated together !
  One so laborious and large, one so refined and so small ;
Singular, too, to reflect—these young folk facing each other,
  He no effeminate man, she a most womanly maid—   1330
Curious, I say, to reflect that the hands were not as their owners :
  That which was small and refined, slender and soft, was the man's ;
That which was clumsy and coarse, and big, was the hand of the maiden !
  He was the lady, it seem'd ; *she* was the muscular man.
Have you not noticed this thing—this strange pathetic *bouleversement*,
  Making our culture and class stronger than Nature and sex ?
Desinit in piscem mulier formosa supernè—
  While from his homelier *couche* Man rises tender and fair !
So that a well-bred youth, fastidious, gracious, and gentle,
  Lives in his delicate world, beauty around him at will,   1340
While some poor maid of the house, as gentle by nature as he is,
  Grows, through hard labour, unfit even to wait upon *him*.
This is an evil, you say ? I respectfully beg to deny it :
  'Tis not an evil at all : 'tis but the half of a good.
She by her labour shall gain self-reliance and strength, as a man does :
  He, through his culture, shall share her inexhaustible grace.

So—let the man be refined, highly organised, even a poet,
    And let the woman be coarse, wholly subdued to her work :
Yet, when her love-time comes, and her motherhood after her marriage,
    Nature asserts itself then—sex has its rights in the end.   1350

BUT I am leaving those two, Mr. Frank and our Dolly, together ;
    He with her hand in his !   What, is he holding it still ?
No—for the moment he felt the touch of her labouring fingers,
    And, looking down at her hand, judged of it there by his own,
Straightway he dropp'd it, and cried, ' Good God, what a hand for a woman !
    ' Where have you lived, all your life ?   What sort of work have you done ? '
Dorothy was not surprised, nor hurt, nor even offended ;
    Only amused, in her way—seeing the change in his tone ;
And she look'd up, and replied, ' I've lived i' one place all my life, Sir ;
    ' And, for my work, I can do all that belongs to a farm :   1360
' I can hoe turnips and wheat ; and plough (as you saw me) and harrow ;
    ' Fettle both horses and cows ; clean out the stable and byre ;
' Milking, of course, I can do ; and poultry and pigs, and the dairy ;
    ' Reaping in harvest time ; haymaking, stacking, an' all—
' And for indoors, I clean, and scrub, and attend to the housework ;
    ' Washing and ironing, too ; baking and brewing, sometimes ;
' Cleaning of knives and boots '—and she look'd courageously at him,
    Looking as one who should say, ' *there* ! would you like any more ? '
He, as he heard, stood amazed ; such a horribly frank revelation,
    Made by so handsome a girl, stagger'd him quite, for awhile !   1370
Then he exclaim'd, ' How strange !   I really can *not* understand you—
    ' Such a sweet face as yours—such indescribable hands !
' What, do you *like* such work ? '   ' Yes, I do, Sir ! I wouldn't exchange it,
    ' No, nor my hands, if I might—not for such soft ones as yourn ! '—
She was grown bold, you perceive ; she had no more fear of his passion :
    Passion ? the touch of her hands cured him completely of love !

Ah, she could talk to him now : she knew that his feelings were alter'd :
     He, with his soft pink palm smarting from pressure of hers !
'Well, pretty Dolly,' he said, 'I must leave you, I fear, to your work, then :
     'Tell me your name, though, at least—I shall not vex you again !'   1380
'*Crump* is my name, Sir,' she said : 'at least, Bessy Crump was my mother :
     'I have no name, only hers ; that's why I hid it, afore.'
'Oh—I perceive ! You are wise ; and don't you be fool'd, like your mother :
     'Marry some honest good man, one in your own rank of life ;
'One who—ahem ! can admire and appreciate hands such as yours are—
     'Hands that can labour for love, doubtless, as well as for hire !'
Labour for love, did he say ? She look'd in his face as he said it—
     Labour for love ? Yes, indeed—that was the wish of her heart !
He had divined it ! And now, she felt so free and so grateful,
     If he had sent her a mile, she would have gone for him twain.   1390
'Ah, your eyes brighten !' said he ; 'but your smiles are for somebody else, though—
     'You have a sweetheart, I see ; you are expecting him now.'
'No, Sir !' poor Dolly replied ; 'oh no, indeed I am not, Sir !
     'But you was speaking so kind—not as you was at the first—
'Gentlefolks *can* do us good, if they keep their place, and advise us—
     'And I am thankful, I sure, if you think kindly o' me !
'Sir, I must go, if you please—my Missis is wanting her supper ;
     'And there's the things to wash up : humbly I wish you good-bye.'
He did not ask for her hand—not again—'twas too dreadful to think of—
     You might as well shake hands with a macadamized road !   1400
But with a kindly farewell he acknowledged her reverent curtsey,
     Watch'd her departing, and then—lighted another cigar.

'Eh, what a blessing,' she thought, as she ran down the lane in the twilight,
     'Eh, what a mercy it was, him getting hold o' my hand !
'But, I was sure it 'd do—for gentlefolks cannot abide 'em—
     'Hardworking hands like mine : theirn is so *very* unlike !

' My, what a hand his was—as soft an' as tender as satin !
  'What must a *lady's* be, if there's such hands in a *man*?'
Thus she ran on ; and the night, coming quietly down into evening,
  Deepen'd the twilight below, lighted the stars up above ;   1410
And she saw no one ; until, by the hayricks close to the farmyard,
  Somebody call'd from behind, ' Dolly, my lass, is it you?'
Ah ! she should know that voice : but it couldn't be *he* though—of course not !
  They hadn't come—and besides, what could she be to him now ?
Still, she must answer and stop—and she trembled a bit, as she did so ;
  Wishing it mightn't be *him* : wishing it might, all the same.

' Oh, Mr. Robert, it's *you ?* Whoever 'ud think for to see you
  ' Standing out here by yourself?   Master 'll take it unkind !
' When did you come ? '—' Why, to-day ; dost think I could wait till to-morrow,
  ' Dolly, thou hard-hearted girl, when I was coming to *thee ?*   1420
' I've got a something to say '—' Oh yes, Mr. Robert, I know it ;
  ' We have heard all—and I sure every one wishes you well ! '
' *Wishes me well*, does she say?   Is the wench gone daft, sin' I left her ?
  ' What have they said about me ?   Dolly, lass, what does thee mean ? '
' Why, Mr. Robert, of course I mean about you an' your wedding ;
  ' Old Mrs. Jellifer came—said it was going to be soon.'—
' *Dang* Mrs. Jelly, I say ! them women must always be meddling !
  ' Dolly, forgive me—I know *thou* wouldn't meddle, for one ! '
' Isn't it true, then ? ' she cried, ' Oh, isn't it true you've a sweetheart ? '
  ' Ay, I've a sweetheart, I hope—that's what I've come about, now :   1430
' But, I can tell how it is—it's Amos, the under-keeper,
  ' Him and his barefooted girl—*that's* how the story began.
' What does it signify, though, the lies they may tell at the Castle ?
  ' Dolly, I've come to fetch *thee !*   Didn't I say I would come ?
' Dolly, thou knows very well I love thee and nobody else, lass—
  ' Hast thou forgotten that night, after our dance, at the farm ? '

'No, Mr. Robert, oh no !' she said, in a tremulous whisper,
   ' Only, I thought you had found somebody better 'an me !'—
' *Somebody better 'an thee ?* Ay, that *would* be a job, though, to find her !
   ' Give me thy hand—that's right—just let me feel it again '—   1440
Freely she gave him her hand ; and not as an antidote this time :
   Sure of an answering grip almost as hard as her own :
' Dolly,' he grasp'd it and said, 'there's lasses a plenty in Scotland ;
   ' Some 'at has hardworking hands, some as are bonny—a few :
' But if there's one on 'em all, for work and for beauty together,
   ' Fit to come second to *thee*—I'm not a keeper, that's all !
'Why, thou must look i' the glass to find such another as thine is—
   ' Such a sweet face, I mean : just like a peach i' the sun !
'And, if thy hands are hard—and I know they couldn't be harder,
   ' Doing such things as thee does, working so hard on the farm—   1450
' *I* like 'em better for that ; for it's real honest labour has done it :
   ' And they'll grow softer in time ; yes, they'll improve by-and-by ! '—
' No, Mr. Robert, they won't ! They shall never be soft, if I know it :
   ' Didn't you tell me yourself I should be glad they was hard ?
' And, do you think, if I'm proud o' the name of a hard-working servant,
   ' I could sit idle at home, when I am—anything else ? '
' Idle, dear Dolly ? Oh no ; it isn't in *thee* to be idle !
   ' Thou shall have work o' thy own, if thou'll be guided by me :
' Give us thy other hand '— and he held up its thick third finger—
   ' Thou's never yet had a ring ; couldn't thee do with one, *here ?* '   1460
' Oh, Mr. Robert,' she cried, ' oh, what shall I say ? I believe you ;
   ' Yes, I believe you indeed ; you are so friendly and kind !
' And I have known you for long—but then, I am only a servant ;
   ' Haven't a penny to give—all as I've got i' the world
' Is just the wages I earn, an' a few little pounds o' my savings ;
   ' How can I do it, you know ? How can I let you love *me* ?
' Oh, it'd be such a shame, if *I* was the one to disgrace you—
   ' You, that's head-keeper an' all ; ay, an' a house o' your own !

E

' You, that has but to speak out, an' there's many a farmer's daughter,
  ' Many a bettermost girl, gladly 'ud have you, I sure ! '
' Oh, you innocent lass ! What signifies farmers' daughters,
  ' Bettermost girls, and that, when I'm a-courting o' *thee ?*
' *Thou* art the one as I want ; an' if any one else would ha' had me,
  ' Why, let 'em whistle, say I : *somebody's* sure to be near !
' Dolly, dear Dolly, say Yes, and come to the house as you talk on,
  ' Come, an' thou'll make it a *home* ; that's what it's never been yet !—'

Did she say Yes ? Who knows ? I don't think any one heard it :
  But he caress'd her unblamed—caught her, and kiss'd her, and held :
She, the stout stalwart wench, with the ample waist, and the shoulders,
  Lay on his heart for awhile, happy and still, like a child.
Where were her strong brown arms, all used to the farm and the cattle ?
  Ah, they were tenderly wreathed, just as a lady's might be :
Where was her sunburnt cheek, all roughen'd and bronzed by the rude winds
  Ah, it was glowing and soft ; warm with ineffable joy :
Even her hands, that had grown to be implements merely of labour,
  Thrill'd with a daintier sense, here in this dreamland of Love !
For, when the love-time comes, the day of delight and possession,
  Out of the loving heart all that is lovely appears ;
All that is sensitive opes—and the signs of labour and sorrow
  Shrink away into the past, counting for nothing at all.
Silent they both of them were, for it was the moment of silence :
  Even in commonplace moods peasants have not many words ;
And at a time like this the most eloquent passion is speechless :
  Language can never express half that humanity feels ;
Yea, and the tongue of the wise, and the rapturous words of the poet,
  Could not deliver in full even poor Dorothy's heart.
Music alone can do that : behold how the mighty Beethoven,
  When Leonora at length clings to her own Florestan,

He, in that hour of supreme transcendent passionate triumph,
 Lifts his immortal airs quite from the region of words ;   1500
Gives to the lovers a cry—inarticulate utterance only,
 Keeps, for the height of his theme, pure and unsyllabled sound.

MUSIC ! There's little of that in the life of an English peasant :
 Dorothy knew not a note—knew not what melody means ;
Yet she could sing—in church ; and doubtless, doubtless, to-morrow
 She will be carolling loud, light'ning her labour with song.
But for to-day, 'twas enough to lean on his breast and be thankful :
 Wondering if it were true, if she were really his own :
Till, in the heart of her joy, in the midst of that tender endearment,
 She was reminded that Love is but a stranger on earth ;   1510
She, so transfigured, refined, to a loftier level of being,
 Fell in a moment, alas ! down to her kitchen again.
For there were voices and lights, and Missis herself in the doorway,
 Over the wide farmyard calling to some one aloud,
' Where can the wench have gone? She's never come back from the cows yet !
 ' Something's amiss, I'll be bound ; 'tisn't like Dolly, at all ! '
Then they both started, those two, where they stood in the dusk by the hayricks :
 ' Oh, Mr. Robert,' she cried, ' Missis is talking o' me !
' I never thought o' the time—I must run, I haven't a minute—
 ' Oh, but to leave you out here, all in the dark, and alone ! '— 1520
' Never you fret about me,' and he kiss'd her lips as he loosed her ;
 ' Leave me alone, lass, for that ; I shall be here again soon :
' Run, Dolly, run— ' and she ran, through the gate, through the yard, through the
 Into the kitchen ; and there, blushing, awaited her doom. [back-door
' Dolly,' said Missis, ' I say ! what's matter? what makes thee so late, girl ? '
 But, as the culprit paused, framing some feeble reply,

Came such a fury of knocks, unexpected, ill-timed, at the front door—
  Door never open'd at all, save on a company day !
'Mercy ! What's that?' cried the dame ; 'one 'ud think they was banging the
  house down.
  ' Happen, my Lady is ill—maybe, the Castle's a-fire !   1530
' Ay, it's bad news, I'll awand !' and she flew to discover the wonder,
  Leaving poor Dolly alone, trembling at such a reprieve.
Mary had run for the door, but her mother achieved it before her ;
  Crying ' Who's there?' till the bolts gave at the voice of a friend.
'Why, Mr. Robert !   Good Lord, is it you, 'at we thought was in Scotland ?
  ' Fraying a body like this !   What, is there anything wrong?'
' Nay, nothing wrong,' said the swain, ' if so be as you take to it kindly—'
  ' *Kindly* be shiver'd !   Come in—Master shall welcome you home.'
' No, not the Master !   It's you, only *you*, as I wanted to speak to,
  ' If you can spare me the time, just a few minutes, alone.'   1540
So they went into the room, the prim little calico parlour,
  Kept like a raree-show ; sacred to holiday times.
There, in the dark (but the moon shone lovingly in through the window)
  Robin unburden'd his mind ; spake of his Dolly, at last :
Spake with a faltering tongue ; for he privily thought that Miss Mary—
  Or, 'twas her mother, perhaps—squinted a little on *him* :
But, as the tale went on, his heart and his masculine courage
  Rose with the theme, and he spake fearless and frank, like a man.
' So,' at the last he said, ' if you think you could any ways spare her,
  ' We might be wed very soon—leastways, in winter, I mean.   1550
' Dolly's a woman grown ; and me, why I'm close upon thirty,
  ' Time to be wed ! and, you know, I can afford her a home.'
All through his tale, ill at ease, making brief exclamations of wonder,
  Lifting her hands and her eyes, sat the incredulous dame ;
Now a believer, at length, in the truth of his misplaced affection ;
  Now a believer ; and yet marvelling how it could be.

' Well, this *is* news !' she exclaim'd, when the story was finally ended ;
  ' Dolly's in wonderful luck, getting a sweetheart like *you* !
' Who would ha' thought it o' *you*, to be choosing a rough farm-servant,
  ' One as is base-born, too !   Not as I blame her for that :
' 'Tisn't her fault, poor thing !   An' I *will* say this for our Dolly,
  ' She is a rare good lass—hardworking, honest, and true :
' But, she's a servant, you know : Mr. Robert, you might ha' done better—
  ' Better a thousand times—ay, and wi' money, an' all !
' Well, she's a handsome face, though I reckon its brown, to our Mary's ;
  ' Ay, and a kind heart too ; *that* I would never deny !
' Yes, and what is it to me, if you fancy a wench o' the kitchen ?
  ' Though she's been here from the first—born in our garret, you know—
' Born ?   Ay, and been like a child, like our own, to me an' my master ;
  ' All her life, you may say : scarce like a servant at all !   1570
' Still, I've no call to say No ; how should I ? she isn't my daughter :
  ' Betsy, her mother, is dead : as for the father, who knows ?
' *I* know him, though, who he is ; he's a gentleman, *that* you may swear to—
  ' Dolly herself shows that, everywhere—even her hands—
' But, if I catch him again, if I ever set eyes upo' *that* man,
  ' He shall ha' something fro' me—some little piece o' my mind !
' Well—for this sweethearting job : deary me, I was almost forgetting—
  ' So, you've a mind to be wed soon, when the winter comes on ?
' *Spare her*, said you ?   If I know I never shall get such another,
  ' What can I do but spare ?   If you must have her, you must !'—   1580
So it was settled ; and he, springing up from his chair, in the moonlight,
  Thank'd her with heartfelt words ; squeezed her warm hand in his own.
' Nay, never thank me !   She's free, and *somebody* 'd sure to ha' had her ;
  ' And, she'll be appy wi' you : *you'll* make her happy, I know.'

Dolly meanwhile, left alone, was standing forlorn in the kitchen ;
  Too much excited to work—too overjoy'd to sit down.

Tearful and silent, she stood ; leaning back on the old oak dresser ;
  Folding her hands on her lap, waiting again for her doom.
Enter to her, unannounced, with a smile full of meaning, Miss Mary :
  Springs to her side, to her cheek : gives her a sisterly kiss !   1590
That was an honour, of course—young Missis a-kissing the servant :
  Dorothy felt it, and blush'd : ' Thank you, Miss Mary,' she said—
' Thank you—I know you mean well ; but I'd liefer it hadn't have happen'd.'
  ' Happen'd ? Why, *what* ? ' cried the girl ; ' how did you know he was here ? '
' Here !' scream'd poor Dolly, ' What, now ? Mr. Robert has come to the house, then ? '
  ' Ay, that he has ! An' what's more, mother herself let him in !
' Yes, she has got him alone, their two sweet selves in the parlour ;
  ' Talking—you know what about : all about sweethearts, an' *you*.
' Didn't I tell you he'd come ? An' didn't I say he was faithful ?
  ' Tell me now—wasn't it *him* kept you so long out o' doors ? '   1600
' Yes, it was him—it was him—I never expected to meet him :
  ' Oh, what a trouble it is, being so happy as this ! '
' *Trouble*, you fainthearted wench ? What, a trouble to marry your sweetheart ?
  ' That's what it's coming to, now ; mother is sure to give in ;
' And you deserve him, you do— ' ' Oh no !' interrupted our Dolly—
  ' Yes, you deserve him, I say—never you tell me you don't !
' So, you'll be happy at last : and *won't* we all come to your wedding !
  ' Come to your wedding, said I ? Nay, you'll be married from here.'
Thus they discoursed ; and anon, the door being furtively open'd,
  Enter bold Robin himself—smiling, successful, and shy :   1610
Shy, when he saw who was there ; and it would have been certainly awkward,
  But that Miss Mary advanced—Nature instructed her so—
Gracious, with offer'd hand, and said, ' Well indeed, Mr. Robert !
  ' Why did you keep it so close ? *You* might ha' trusted us all ! '
Soothed by her tact—for it show'd she was not disappointed, nor jealous—
  Robert shook hands like a friend ; thank'd her, and tried to explain :
But she withdrew ; for she said, ' *Two's* company, isn't it, Dolly ?
  ' *Three* isn't wanted just now : so, Mr. Robert, good-night ! '

Lightly she left them alone, like a wise and sensible maiden :
  So did her mother, awhile : so will we too, if you please !   1620
For there's another thing still, one more little episode wanting,
  Ere we can leave them for good,—husband (it may be) and wife.   1622

END OF BOOK II.

BOOK III.

'TWAS on that very same night, in the smoking-room at the Castle,
  After the ladies had gone, sorely fatigued, to their rest—
For they had suffer'd a ball, poor things, and an archery meeting,
  Also a ride in the park, all within twenty-four hours—
'Twas on the very same night ; and our great Parliamentary Colonel
  Sat with his nephew, alone, over a final cigar.
Even their host had retired ; Sir Harry, the pink of politeness,
  Left his dear cousins, and left brandy and soda and all ;
He, with appropriate words, with courtesies apologetic,
  Hoped they'd forgive him, for once : ' Damnable headache, you know ! '
Thus they were seated alone ; and the talk was of racing and hunting,
  Gossip, and girls, and game—all that Society loves.
Suddenly, Frank broke out—' I say though, talking of shooting,
  ' Do you remember that girl out in the open, at plough ?
' Well, I have seen her again.' ' What of that ? ' quoth the excellent Colonel ;
  ' You are too wise, I presume, *twice* to commit yourself there ! '
' Oh yes ! But I was obliged, as luck would have it, to meet her ;
  ' For she was driving her cows up to the gate where I was.
' So, I just ask'd how she did ; said a few sage words on the weather ;
  ' Nothing that *could* do her harm—Virtue, and you, were my guard !
' True, I was somewhat impress'd by her beautiful eyes, and her features :
  ' Brown as she is, there's *finesse*—yes, there's real beauty, in them.

' But there's an antidote near ; her hands are so painfully horny,
  ' Eros himself wouldn't dare lay his soft finger on hers ! '—
' Well then—*et puis* ? What's the point of this very remarkable story ? '—
  ' Ah, you may laugh—but I'm sure something uncommon there is !
' How should a peasant like her, so coarse and repulsive in some things,
  ' Have such a highbred face ; gentle, serene, and refined ?   1650
' Uncle, why even your *Bill to Regulate Female Employment*
  ' Doesn't explain such a thing : trust me, it doesn't indeed ! '
' *You* can explain it, then, eh ? ' ' Why, yes, if you'll only have patience :
  ' She is a charity child, born on the farm where she lives ;
' And, although *she* doesn't know, I'm sure her anonymous father
  ' Must have been some one of rank : some one superior, at least.'—
' What a romance ! And where is your hard-handed heroine's dwelling ?
  ' Where does she slumber at eve, after her feats at the plough ?
' Has she a highsounding name, *à propos* to her lofty condition ? '—
  ' *Dorothy Crump* is her name—that is plebeian enough !   1660
' White Rose Farm is the house ; that pretty old house by the river—
  ' Don't you remember the cliff, just at the turn of the road ?
' Dorothy Crump is her name : I ask'd, and she artlessly told me :
  ' But, 'tis her mother's, of course ; *that* is no clue to her birth.'—
' White Rose Farm, did you say ? ' said the languid Colonel, arising ;
  Shaken, it seem'd, for a time out of his evening repose :
' Well, 'tis a charming name ! And the story is just as you put it—
  ' Folly has father'd her face : labour accounts for her hands.
' But, it is late ; Cousin Hal is sleeping the sleep of the blessed :
  ' Bedtime, my boy ! ' And they went each to his bachelor room.   1670

ODDLY enough—next day, for the first time since his arrival,
  Colonel St. Quentin went out, long before breakfast, alone.
It was a beautiful morn ; the first white frost of October
  Sharpen'd the autumn air, freshen'd the odours of earth,

Shed upon leafage and lawn its crisp white gossamer garment,
　　Thin as a bridal veil; sparkling, and snowy, and cold.
Where then, so early a-field, this beautiful maidenly morning,
　　Sacred to innocent peace, pure as the breast of a bride,
Where did the Colonel go?—Who knows? Perhaps to the stables?
　　Or to the kennels, beyond? Or, for a stroll, to the Lodge? 　　　1680
Or to the river, perchance? Ah yes! No doubt, to the river;
　　For 'twas at White Rose Farm somebody saw him go by.
But, he return'd in time to behold, in the private garden,
　　Roses, late roses, in hand, Lady Sophia herself.
'Ah!' cried the gallant M.P., 'what happiness, Lady Sophia,
　　'Thus to surprise you, for once, here in your Eden, alone!'—
'Nay, Cousin Charles,' said the Dame, with a stately and courteous Goodmorrow,
　　'If I am Eve at her flowers, who, may it please you, are *you*?'
'Not, I assure you, a snake! Oh no, I have no such intentions:
　　'You have already attain'd all that an Eve could desire. 　　　1690
'*I* have no apples to give, and you are omniscient without them:
　　'*'*Tis not for me to aspire—*I* cannot hope to persuade:
'No—*mais le père de famille, c'est lui, c'est monsieur votre mari—*
　　'*Capable, celui-là, de tout;* even of charming his wife!'—
That was a neat little touch; for he knew she was fond of Sir Harry:
　　Fond of him still—how strange! after a dozen of years:
Some ladies are, I perceive, thus cold and disdainful to others,
　　Keeping a soft little heart warm for their husbands alone.
Therefore, she brighten'd the more; and answer'd, with elegant fervour,
　　'Ah, Cousin Charles, you are still subtle and smooth, as of old! 　　　1700
'Well for the women at large you are now so devoted to serve them;
　　'If you took opposite views, what would become of us all?
'Tell me—your excellent *Bill to Regulate Female Employment,*
　　'How does it work, *mon ami*, on the Conservative mind?
'How are the Liberals pleased with that useful idea of coercion,
　　'Telling a woman to do just what men say, and no more?

' That wouldn't answer, of course, in the higher spheres of employment :

   ' We must be absolute there—quite independent of *you* !

' But, for the lower, 'tis well; they have too much freedom already ;

   ' Working, like men almost, out in the open, alone !   1710

' Would you believe—there are girls, yes, *girls*, on this very estate here,

   ' Getting their living a-field, following horses at plough !

' Is it not dreadful, to think of such gross, unfeminine conduct ?

   ' Yet they are actually fond—*fond*, of such labour as that !

' They have been told it is wrong ; but what is the use of our telling?

   ' Nothing can stop it but you—you, and your excellent Bill.

' Oh—*à propos* of these girls, my housekeeper tells me this morning

   ' We have a little romance here, on the premises, now !

' You condescend, I know, to the poor and their lowly enjoyments :

   ' You too, perhaps, can endure Robin the keeper's romance ?   1720

' Come—as we walk to the house, for I see it is breakfast time, nearly—

   ' I will discourse you of love ; love at the tail of the plough !

' Robin, you know—Robin George, Sir Harry's respected head keeper ?

   ' Such a head keeper, it seems, never was seen upon earth !

' Even in Scotland, forsooth, my husband must have his assistance,

   ' Though you and Frank would arrive *days* before he could return.

' Well—Robert George has a house, of course, and an excellent income ;

   ' Therefore, the women supposed he must be wanting a wife.

' He, a fine well-to-do man, on the right side of thirty, or near it,

   ' Sends a soft flutter of love all through the dovecotes around.   1730

' Every fair creature whose rank was sufficiently high and exalted,

   ' Thought (so they tell me) at length *she* might become Mrs. George !

' Farmers' daughters, to wit—upper servants here at the Castle—

   ' Tradesfolk in yonder town—schoolmistress there at the Glebe—

' Ah, 'twas a mere travestie of what happens with *us*, when a hero,

   ' Blest with his ample estate, swoops on the county at large !

' One sweet nymph, it was thought, our Robert especially favour'd ;

   ' Mary of White Rose Farm : don't you delight in the name?

' Most respectable girl—so they tell me, I never have seen her—
   ' Money—an only child—really a suitable match !   1740
' So that the rest, with a sigh and a shudder at Cupid's caprices,
   ' Left him alone with his choice, gave him permission to woo.
' Thus it went on ; but to-day—oh, horror of horrors—the news is
   ' 'Tis not Mary at all ; Robin refuses her love !
' 'Tis but a servant of theirs, a bondager bred on the homestead—
   ' Some coarse creature, no doubt, following horses at plough.
' Fancy, how shame and disgust run wild in the hearts of my maidens !
   ' Women, you know, Cousin Charles, all are alike about this :
' How should I feel—yes, and *you*—if some upstart citizen's daughter
   ' Tangled dear Frank in her toils, forced the poor boy to propose?   1750
' Still, 'tis amusing enough, that grades so trivial in *our* eyes
   ' Seem to the vulgar so large : what does it matter, at all,
' Whether a keeper like George shall marry a farmer's daughter,
   ' Or, a few levels below, stoop to the lowest of all ?
' So, I have taken his part ; for the girl, they confess, is goodlooking—
   ' And I have views about that, even in cases like hers—
' *I* have condoned his offence ; so the world must be pleased to be tranquil :
   'Even my housekeeper's tongue soon will begin to applaud !
' Nay, I have *sanction'd* the girl : for Robert has orders to bring her
   ' Up to the Castle to-day, here to be judged and approved.   1760
' Ah, by the way—if you like, you may witness that touching *dénoûment* :
   ' Something may int'rest you there ; something germane to the Bill !'

Grave and polite as he was, an attentive listener always,
   Int'rested really, it seem'd, e'en in so homely a tale,
Colonel St. Quentin at last had certainly fretted a little ;
   Just at the end—at the words ' here to be judged and approved.'
Haply, he thought to himself, ' Who cares for the loves of a keeper?
   ' He and his lubberly wench, why should they trouble us here ?'

But, in his features composed, in his train'd and tutor'd expression,
   Nothing so rude could appear ; everything beam'd, as it ought,   1770
Bicker'd and beam'd with delight—acquiescence disguised in effusion—
   ' It was a charming idea ; yes, he would certainly come.'—
They were arrived at the house, at the beautiful garden-entrance ;
   He, with a cousinly grace aptly enforced by a smile,
Handed her Ladyship in, to the wainscoted oak, to the armour ;
   Just as the gong had begun, handed her into the hall.

LEAVE we them thus, with the guests, with the late luxurious breakfast :
   We to their exquisite joys may not presume to aspire ;
We must go down to the farm, to White Rose Farm in the valley,
   Whither, on errands of love, Robin already has gone.
He, with a mind confused, with a heart all troubled within him,
   Went on his errand of love : gladly he hasted to go ;
But, to be *sent*, to perceive that his sweetheart must come to be stared at—
   That was a doubtful thing ; what should he think about that ?
' Surely, my Lady means well—she means for to do us an honour—
   ' And, for myself, I am glad ; glad to have Dorothy seen ;
' So as the gentles may know, let alone them gossiping servants,
   ' She is a jewel, and worth—well, say a dozen o' *them !*
' But, she won't like it, I know ; she's afeard o' the housekeeper, even ;
   ' What'll she think, to be brought straight to my Lady herself ?·   1790
' Ay, and they'll stare at her clothes, at her hands, at her simple behaviour—
   ' 'Gad, I had liefer by half meet wi' yon poachers, alone ! '—
Thus while he walk'd in his mood, lo, Dolly herself stood before him :
   She from a hedge close by sprang, with a hoe in her hand ;
For she had finish'd her work in the field, and was off to her dinner,
   Ready—alas, how depraved ! ready for bacon and beer.
' Oh, Mr. Robert, what, *you* ? '   ' Why, Dolly, my lassie, my darling ! '
   Few are the words that precede warm salutations of love :

Kisses—how novel and sweet are the first that follow betrothal !
　　Press'd upon lips that are now—yes, and for ever, your own.　　　　1800
But, when their rapture was done (for it is but a fleeting enjoyment)
　　Robin bethought him with pain how he should speak to the maid ;
How he should break the bad news, the tale of that terrible order,
　　Bidding her come, and so soon, up to Sir Harry's with him.
'Dolly, love, don't be afeard !　You and me are to go the Castle,
　　' Just for an outing, you know—just for a bit of a spree ;
' And I am glad, for I know there isn't a girl o' the servants—
　　' No, nor the ladies as well, fit to be reckon'd wi' you ! '—
'*Go to the Castle!*' she cried, ' What for ?　Oh no, Mr. Robert—
　　' I canna do it, indeed—specially, going wi' *you* !　　　　　　1810
' What would the housekeeper say, and the ladies' maids, and the housemaids ?
　　' Me to go trolloping there, bringing you trouble and shame !'—
'Never you mind what they say ; and it isn't the housekeeper, neither :
　　' Dolly, my Lady herself wants to set eyes upon *you* !
'And, when she sees you so fair, in your Sunday frock and your bonnet,
　　' If she don't take to you *then*, I'll never trust her no more !'—
Ah, it was vain, that appeal to the natural weakness of woman :
　　Dolly's blue eyes were all dim—dim with her troublesome tears.
'*What* !' she exclaim'd—'what, me, to go and be shown to my Lady !
　　' *Me* !' and she look'd at her clothes, look'd at her hardworking hands :　1820
'Oh, I should sink i' the earth !　Mr. Robert, you shouldn't have let her—
　　' She'd never wish it, I'm sure, if she could see what I am.
' Oh, get me off, if you can, get me off, for I couldn't abide it !
　　' Why, it might lose you your place, having a sweetheart like me !'—
' Lose me my place ?' said the swain, 'and because I have *you* for a sweetheart !
　　' Marry come up, no indeed !　Nay, I shall make it secure ;
' If she has sense, she must see what a wife you will make for a keeper,
　　' Fit for to help him abroad, fit to be happy at home.
' But, you must come : for she said I must bring you myself to the Castle :
　　' Them was her positive words !　Dolly, you'll do it for *me* ?'—　　1830

What can a woman refuse to the man whom she loves—to her master,
    So he be worthy to rule, so he be gentle and kind?
Then, his more equable strength, his masculine width of horizon,
    Justify her to herself, yielding her wishes to his;
Specially, if she should feel, as Dorothy felt in her meekness,
    Being so young and so low, sadly unworthy of him.
Dolly was strong as a horse—so the girls of the village would tell you—
    And she was tall as a man; muscular, massive, and firm
All through her large live limbs; self-reliant in character, also,
    Needing no help in her work, asking for nothing—save love.   1840
Yet, being such and so strong, a rough undisciplined servant,
    Able to fend for herself, used to act freely alone,
Now that fair Eros was come, and had learn'd her the lore of a lover,
    She was as weak as the rest : mild as a minikin maid.
Strange, when her great hard hand lay in his, as light as a lady's !
    Strange, when her stalwart frame lean'd on his breast, like a child !
Strange? Not at all ! 'Twas the sure, the instinctive teaching of Nature,
    Guiding the woman at once straight to the heart of the man.
So, she has yielded at last : but tearfully still, and in terror ;
    Dreading those gorgeous grandees lying in wait at the Squire's ;   1850
Dreading the smart sleek maids, and the gentlefolks, chiefly the ladies ;
    Dreading supremely, of course, Lady Sophia herself.
Robert will stand by her side? She falters a little, in asking :
    She will be near him, at least? Only, a little behind—
Yes, just a little behind ; out of sight of the strangers, or nearly ;
    Close to the doorway ; and so ready at once to escape?
'Oh, but they'll speak to you, lass ; they'll ask you a few little questions :'
    Speak? What a terrible thought ! If she were forced to reply,

Could he not do it instead?   He was used to the ways of the gentry :
  Couldn't he answer for her, saying—whatever he liked?—   1860
Yes, he has promised it all ; has fondly, egregiously promised
  All that his Dolly could ask : more than he dared to perform.

SOON—for they hurried along, each wrapt in thoughts of the other,
  And of those mighty events coming so near to them both—
Soon, they arrived at the farm ; in time for the noonday dinner.
  Little cared Dorothy, now, either for bacon or beer :
But, when her mistress observed (having heard the great news of the summons)
  ' If the fond lass won't eat, nothing can come o' the job,'
She, with her heart in her mouth, sat down to the mug and the trencher,
  And, with an effort, at length finish'd her morsel of food.   1870
For, they had given her leave ; and as for the afternoon milking,
  Foddering, feeding the pigs—Mary would see to all that.
Was it not kind? Dolly thought : so like her Missis and Mary !
  Happen what might at the Squire's, *they* would be friends to her still.
So, with a lighter heart, she went up anon to her attic ;
  Minded to deck herself out all in her very best things.
Partly, for vanity?   Well, who would dare to say *No*, with a woman?
  And, of her face and her form, Dolly had cause to be vain :
But, of her treasures, ah no ! so rarely, so briefly, she wore them,
  New as they look'd, they were old ; old both in fashion and age.   1880
Dorothy knew it quite well : even *she* had an eye for the fashions :
  But she had nothing, save these ; they were her best, and her all.
Partly for vanity, then, if you will, and partly for duty,
  Yet, if I know her at all, chiefly she wore them for love ;
Not for the gentles alone, and to show her respect for my Lady—
  That was a duty, of course—but, she was going with *him* :
And, if indeed she were his, indeed acknowledged a sweetheart,
  She, with such honours in view, *must* look as well as she can.

So that ere long she came down, in her brown straw cottager's bonnet,
   Graced with a little white cap circling her beautiful face ;   1890
Graced too with ribbons—a bow at the side, and strings, and a curtain—
   Over her sunburnt neck spreading their virginal blue :
Came in her green plaid shawl, with its soft vague chequer of purple :
   Came in her russet-grey frock, modestly made and severe ;
Sleeved to the wrists, of course ; descending quite to the ankles ;
   Not, like her everyday wear, kilted half way to the knee :
Came in her best black boots ; not heavy with earth and with iron,
   Huge, and unfit for the house, such as she commonly wore ;
But a diminutive pair—not much too big for the Colonel ;
   Black'd (she had taken such pains) almost as brightly as his.—   1900
Such was her dress : for her face, it was rosy and fresh as the morning ;
   Brown—like a cairngorm stone set in the gold of her hair :
Delicate pale soft gold, lying smooth on her sun-smitten temples,
   Lighting the dusk of her cheek, rippling away to her ears.
Ornaments ? Nay, she had none ; save the brooch she had fasten'd her shawl with:
   'Twas Mr. Robert's last gift, bought at the Martlemas Fair.
Oh—and her collar and cuffs : but, alas! they were *not* ornamental ;
   They were a contrast, a foil, deep'ning the hue of her skin ;
Surfaces polish'd and white, with the fine smooth texture of linen,
   Close to her sun-tann'd face, close to her rough, ruddy hands !   1910
' *That* winna do,' thought the dame ; 'she looks browner and coarser than ever ;
   ' Yet she's goodlooking, I swear ; ay, she's as bonny as good !'
' Dolly,' she utter'd aloud, ' thou's fettled thysen to a T, lass !
   ' But, there is one thing still ; hanna thee got any *gloves* ? '
' Gloves ? ' cried poor Dolly, aghast ; ' why, Missis, they baffle my hands so !
   ' I never wear 'em, you know ; scarce of a Sunday, at church !
' But there's a pair upstairs, i' my box—I know it is somewheres—
   ' Maybe they'll do for to-day ; if I can still get 'em on.'
It was that old yellow pair, that were once her anonymous father's ;
   Left, by some chance, at the farm : sole reminiscence of him.   1920

'Run for 'em, lass, ay; do !   It'll look more respectful to wear 'em ;
   '*I* know the gentlefolks' ways : happen they'd notice thy hands.'
Robert had noticed them too ; but herself was the thing that he cared for ;
   He was enamour'd of that—therefore, of everything else :
And, as she stood there, he thought he never had seen her so charming ;
   Cleanly and sweet as she was, fit to be Queen of the May.
When she came back with the gloves, and he kiss'd her (by leave of her Missis),
   'Isn't she bonny ?' he cried ; 'isn't she fit for a lord ?
'If there's a man or a maid finds fault with her, up at the Castle,
   'Gentles or not, it's all one—they'll ha' to reckon wi' me !'   1930
Which when the lover had said, with a mind to encourage his sweetheart,
   He with a hearty good-day, she with an anxious farewell,
Bade their adieu to the twain, to the Missis and kindly Miss Mary ;
   Went through the yard, through the croft, up by the path of the hill.

Mother and daughter, the while, look'd after them out of the doorway ;
   Silent at first ; but ere long, briskly the mother bespake :
'Well, 1 could like to be there—I could like to ha' been in among 'em,
   'Just to ha' seen him again ; just to make sure it was him.'—
'*Who*, mother ?'—'Didn't you see, in the lane, quite early this morning,
   'Somebody staring about, dolloping round by the yard ?   1940
'Looking for Dolly, mayhap !   But she wasn't in sight, for a wonder ;
   'She was a-milking, you know ; 'long o' the cows, i' the byre.
'Mary, it's twenty good year—twenty-one, come Mothering Sunday—
   'Since he was here at the farm, him and his dandering ways !
'But, I could tell him at once, though his hair 's got as grey as my master's :
   'Just the same sodgering walk ; eyeglass, moustaches, an' all.
'He'll be some kin at the house ; to Sir Harry, or else to my Lady :
   '*That's* how it is, I'll awand !   He's at the Castle, no doubt.'—
'Eh, what a thing, if it's true !' cried Mary, lost in amazement ;
   'Him at the Castle ?   Why then, surely he'll see her to-day !   1950

'What will he do, do you think? Will he know who she is? Will he own her?

'Well, if he does, only think! Dolly's a lady, at once!'—

'*Own her?*' the Missis replied, 'own Dolly, and make her a lady?

'Ay—make a soft silk purse out of a sow's leather ear!

'Nay, you may trust him, my lass—*he'll* none let 'em see 'at he owns her—

'Let me alone, though, for that; *I* can speak up what I know!'—

'Nay, mother, don't!' said the girl; 'our Dolly knows nothing about it;

'Nor Mr. Robert, of course; nobody knows, but oursels:

'It'd do nothing but harm; for my Lady would never believe it;

'And, if she took it amiss, what'd become o' them two?'   1960

THUS while they fondly discoursed on the chances of Dorothy's birthright,

She and her lover advanced up the steep path of the hill;

Up to the top of the cliff, where the martins build in the springtime;

Up through the hazels beyond; up through the fields, to the park.

There—for already in sight the Castle appear'd in the distance—

There, with a beating heart, Dorothy falter'd and paused:

Wondering how she should look, how behave, in that terrible palace;

Vainly, with fingers untrain'd, striving—to put on her gloves!

They were too small; they were old; they were never intended for *her* hands:

How could her broad hard palm bend to the flexible kid?   1970

'Oh, Mr. Robert,' said she, 'it'll do if I carry 'em, won't it?

'Gloves! They was never, I sure, meant for such creatures as me!

'I'm not ashamed o' my hands; and if *you* don't want me to wear 'em—

'These little pottering things—do let me throw 'em away!'

'Nay, never throw 'em away; never lose a good thing when you've got it;

'But, for your hands, Dolly dear, show 'em and welcome, for me!'

So, with the gloves in her grasp, just to prove that she own'd such a treasure,

Dorothy follow'd her swain up to that dreaded abode:

Up through the stables, and thence by the shrubbery path to the courtyard,
   Where, in their splendid attire, footmen and housemaids appear'd.   1980
Ah, how they stared ! Dolly thought ; and her cheeks grew as red as a rooster,
   Ah, how that bold little maid toss'd up her nose in the air !
But, it was over and done—they were safe in the house, in a moment ;
   Safe in that solemn domain round Mrs. Jellifer's door.
She, Mrs. Jellifer, sat in her sacred though stuffy apartment,
   Thinking of Robert ; in doubt how to behave to his bride :
How to be friendly to him, and still show her teeth at his sweetheart :
   How to be civil, and yet teach the rude hussy her place.
But, with the knock at her door, with the advent of Robert and Dolly,
   All this tremendous intent vanish'd at once into air.   1990
'Twas not the beautiful face ; 'twas the curtsey poor Dorothy made her,
   Which with its artless respect soften'd the heart of the dame.
Shyly then Robert began : ' Mrs. Jellifer, this is my sweetheart ;
   ' Dolly, you know, at the farm ; come for my Lady to see ! '—
' Oh yes, I know,' said the dame : ' and how do you do, Mr. Robert ?
   ' Nay, then—shake hands with a friend, wishes you happy, I'm sure ! '
But, while she gave him her hand, and he wrung it with masculine vigour,
   Dolly came into her mind : must she shake hands too with *her* ?
Nay, that was not in the bond ; and the wench wouldn't dare to expect it :
   Look you, how sheepish she stands, waiting, aback o' the door !   2000
But it was Robert's resolve, that Dorothy shouldn't be slighted :
   So, with the least little wink, least little push from behind,
' Dolly, love, don't be afeard ! ' he said, ' Mrs. Jellifer 's waiting ;
   ' She's been a friend to us both—she's got a welcome for you.'
Honest entrapper of sneaks, courageous destroyer of vermin,
   Macte virtute, my man ! Woman 's outwitted, for once !
For, at his artful appeal, the housekeeper redden'd a little,
   Saw she must do it, and so might as well do it with grace ;
Said, with an affable air, ' Young woman, I see you are lucky—'
   ' Lucky ?' cried Robert, ' Nay, come ! surely, it's *me* 'at's in luck ! '   2010

'*Lucky*, I say,' quoth the dame, 'to ha' got such an excellent husband ;
   ' Which there's a many, my girl, gladly 'ud stand i' your shoes !
' Not but I wishes you well ; ' and she smiled, condescending and gracious ;
   Smiled, and—incredible feat !—boldly extended her hand.
But, when she felt such a palm as Dorothy timidly offer'd,
   Rasping her soft mottled skin e'en with its modest embrace,
Quickly she dropp'd it ; and said, with a start (just a little affected),
   ' You've got a hardworking place, judged by the feel o' your hand ! '
' Yes, ma'am,' said Dolly, ' it is ; it's a hardworking place, but a good one ;
   ' I should be sorry to leave yet, if it wasn't for *him* !   2020
' But, Mr. Robert is kind ; and Missis 'll still be a neighbour ;
   ' I shall be always at hand, ready to help on the farm.'
' Fool ! ' thought the dame : and perhaps she had lectured the girl on her folly,
   But, with a ladylike knock, somebody enter'd the room.—
Ha ! 'tis my Lady herself ! 'tis βοῶπις πότνια Ἥρη,
   Come to observe, to assist, labouring mortals below ;
Come to inspect and approve Briseis, captive and servant :
   Come to behold for herself sturdy Achilles in love !
Gorgeous in afternoon dress, prepared for a drive in the carriage,
   Fresh from the hands of her maid, she, the Immortal, appears :   2030
Clad—but I dare not describe ; for, before you have finish'd describing,
   Out goes the fashion ; and then, 'tis but a vulgar array.
Ah, what a flutter there was, when that glory of velvet and odours,
   Mantled and feather'd and furr'd, enter'd the housekeeper's room !
Foolish Briseis, and fond, sought refuge behind her Achilles,
   Curtseying once and again, deeper than ever before :
E'en Mrs. Jellifer's dress, that was almost as long as my Lady's,
   Show'd, by its faltering folds, something was supple within ;
As for bold Robin, he stood, erect yet wholly respectful ;
   Grave, with a manly regard, lifting a hand to his brow.   2040
But, for the Goddess herself, just come from a luncheon of nectar,
   Down to these commonplace folks, purely from motives of love,

Can we sufficiently praise her majestic matronly manner?
　　Can we—ah, never, alas!—fully express it in words?
No! we must leave that to you, intelligent exquisite reader,
　　You, who have fed on the sweets, lain in the lilies, of life;
You, who can quite understand the vast, the incredible distance
　　Which in a world like ours, orderly, proper, and proud,
Spreads from my Lady on high, the Earl's daughter, the queen of the county,
　　Down to poor Dolly the maid, following horses at plough!　　　　2050
Distance! Her ladyship's dress—her velvet and furs, and her odours,
　　Jewels and feathers and lace, cambric, diminutive gloves—
Oh, what a contrast, you say, to Dolly's short frock and straw bonnet,
　　And to her old plaid shawl, and to her bare rugged hands!
Yes; but the contrast indeed, the antipodean exemplar,
　　Is not alone in the dress—is in the wearers themselves;
One, a strange marvel of art and civilization and culture,
　　Wrought till the natural ground hardly again shall appear;
As for the other, she has common-sense and simplicity only;
　　Nature and Labour alone went to the making of *her*.　　　　2060
But there is somebody else—there is somebody else in the background;
　　Not unattended, it seems, Herè descends from above:
Who can this deity be, with the glossy and tutor'd moustaches,
　　Eyeglass, and soldierly air?—Colonel St. Quentin, by Jove!
Rather surprising, it is, when the great Parliamentary Colonel
　　Swoops from his Liberal bench down to a housekeeper's room!
So Mrs. Jellifer thought; though she didn't quite put it in that way:
　　'As for my Lady,' she thought, 'why, it is all very well;
'But for the Colonel to come prying after a couple o' sweethearts,
　　'That is uncommonly odd, very demeaning to *him!*'　　　　2070
Robert, however, was glad; he had often attended the Colonel,
　　Often been handsomely tipp'd—ay, and deservedly too;
And, with a natural pride, he thought, 'He has heard, from the master,
　　'And, like a gentleman, comes kindly a-wishing us well.'

As for our Dolly, she stared ; she did not remember the Colonel ;
  Curtsey'd and trembled and stared, wondering who it might be :
Thinking that *one* was enough, and *two* was sadly too many :
  ' Gentlefolks coming down here, just to make fun o' poor me !'
Simpleton ! Little she knew of βοῶπις πότνια "Ηρη :
  Little could *she* understand how the Immortals behave !   2080
They were as foreign to her as they will be, ere long, to her betters ;
  When o'er the studies of Youth, Science is voted supreme—
When we have done with the past; and its accurate elegant wisdom ;
  When in all English schools Greek is for ever taboo'd.

NOT with the icy disdain that our ignorant Dolly expected,
  Not with the haughty contempt dear to a Jellifer's heart,
But with a heavenly smile, inexpressibly sweet and superior,
  Helping her low rich voice, thus did the goddess begin :—
' Robert, I see you are come—and Sir Harry expressly desired it—
  ' Here, with the girl of your choice, into a circle of friends !   2090
' For you have served us so well, you have been such an excellent keeper,
  ' We are entitled, you know, thus to be friendly with you.
' And, for myself, I have wish'd to make the young woman's acquaintance,
  ' Knowing how well you deserve all that a woman can give.
' Yes '—and the light of her charms shone full on the tremulous Dolly—
  ' Yes, you are happy, my girl ! And I am sure you are good :
' I have inquired ; I find you have long been an excellent servant ;
  ' So we may justly presume you will do well as a wife.
' Still, I was hardly prepared—I had not been told of your beauty :
  ' Where have you hid it ? and why have I not seen you before ?'—   2100
Why? Pretty question, indeed ! For how should her ladyship notice
  Dolly at work on the farm, Dolly a-field with the plough ?
Ere they had time to reply, the amiable goddess continued—
  ' Is she not handsome, Charles ? Has he not chosen with taste ?

'Yes, you are comely, my child ; I declare, you are beautiful, really !

'And you have sense, I perceive—far too much sense to be vain.

'Tell me your name, and your age ? ' And Dorothy curtsey'd, and told it :

'Ah, 'tis a charming old name ; fresh as the scent of the hay !

'Dorothy, when you come home to your husband's house by the cover,

'I shall inspect you, and see, some day, how happy you are.'   2110

'Thank you, my Lady, I'm sure,' said Robert ; 'that *will* be an honour !'

Dorothy echoed his words—'Thank you, my Lady, I'm sure !'

Thinking, however, far more of that vision of home and a husband,

Offer'd so kindly, and now nearer than ever to her.

'But,' said my Lady once more, 'I must not keep you all standing ;

'You, Mrs. Jellifer, know what I should wish to be done ;

'You have already, no doubt, offer'd tea to your guests—or a supper—

'Not in the servants' hall ; here, in your own pretty room.

'And there is one thing yet : for, Robert, you know at a wedding

'Brides must have everything new, everything proper and smart :   2120

'So '—and she turn'd to the maid—'you must let me make you a present ;

'Something to buy you a dress such as your beauty deserves.'

Then, from a perfumed purse, with gloved and delicate fingers,

Something she drew, with a smile : Dorothy, blushing and brown,

Held out her own poor hand, reluctantly forced to reveal it ;

Curtsey'd and humbly replied, 'Thank you, my Lady,' again.

But when her ladyship's eyes caught sight of poor Dorothy's fingers,

And when the tips of her gloves touch'd that astonishing hand,

Startled, she lifted her brows, and with wonder and horror and pity

Gazed on the grey hard palm, bright with the polish of toil :   2130

Gazed, and look'd up from the hand to the beautiful face of its owner ;

Then from that feminine face back to the labourer's hand :

Seeming about to exclaim, to ask of that terrible contrast :

Checking herself in the act, only for Dorothy's sake—

Dolly, who never observed that fearful, that fatal impression :

Dolly, who, had she been ask'd, would not have minded at all ;

Would but have artlessly said, ' It's work, if you please, ma'am, has done it ;
  ' Work, that has harden'd my hands ; work, that has made 'em so big !'

Now, with this harrowing scene, this sad revelation, before him,
  How did the Colonel behave? What did it please him to do?   2140
He too came forward, and smiled ; and said, ' For the sake of your lover
  ' You must allow me, my girl, some little share in your joy !
' Robert I know and respect ; he will make you a very good husband ;
  'And I may safely predict you'll be an excellent wife :
' So, as a friend to you both—one gladly assured of your welfare—
  ' I would present you with this, merely to purchase the ring.'
Most of his beautiful words (ah me, in the Parliament Chamber,
  How many beautiful words falter unheeded away !)—
Most of his elegant words, in their incomprehensible beauty,
  Pass'd over Dorothy's head, left her as wise as before ;   2150
But she received what he gave—received it in lowly confusion ;
  Curtseying ; murmuring still, ' Thank ye, Sir, thank ye, I'm sure !'
Till, for a crown of the whole, a startling thrilling *finale*,
  Just as my Lady had turn'd, waving a gracious farewell,
' Now,' said the Colonel, ' good-bye ! Although I am almost a stranger,
  ' I must confess that I wish—heartily wish—to shake hands !'
Nay, she was helpless, and cow'd : for the thing was all done in a moment :
  Ere she could beg a reprieve, ere she could utter a word,
He, with an exquisite *pose*, with a graceful, a fatherly *congé*,
  Lifting her hand, had convey'd part of it into his own !   2160
Part of her tell-tale palm in his soft though masculine fingers
  Rested a moment ; and why—why did it make him afraid?
Why did the warrior turn pale, and, his grasp on a sudden relaxing,
  Bid her a hasty adieu, striding away to the door?
Haply, that touch of her hand reveal'd to the affable Colonel
  What a tremendous abyss sever'd our Dolly from him :

Rank, education, mind ; even make and outward appearance,
　All were against her, you see : all, save her beautiful face.
Yet, what of that ?   What else could one ever expect, in a servant?
　Was it not kind, though, of him, taking such interest in *her ?*　　　2170
Or, was it only his *Bill to Regulate Female Employment*
　Made him attentive to her—just to see what she was like ?

WELL, they are gone then, at last ; my Lady, and also the Colonel :
　After such efforts as theirs, sure they are glad to depart :
Ah, what a sense of relief ! for them, to escape from the vulgar ;
　And for the vulgar, alas ! just to be left to themselves.
Good Mrs. Jellifer's tongue was tied by her lofty position ;
　Robert's by duty and pride ; Dolly was modestly mute ;
But in their hearts all three were saying 'Thank goodness, it's over ;
　'Quality's done with us now : now we can talk at our ease !'　　　2180
First, in her ample armchair the housekeeper flung herself, sighing
　' Now, Mr. Robert, sit down ; see, there's another armchair.
' Dolly, you've come like a wife—we must reckon you one of ourselves, lass ;
　'And you've been standing so long : nay, you must really sit down !'
So, in that presence august—an earnest of matronly glories—
　Even our Dolly, although shy and unwilling, sat down ;
And, round the fire, at peace,·they talk'd of the Past and the Future,
　How the great folks had behaved : when should the wedding-day be.
' Dolly,' said Robert at length, ' how much did the gentlefolks give thee ?
　' Thou's getting rich, I'll awand—two wedding presents at once !'　　　2190
' Nay,' said poor Dolly, ' I sure they was nothing but pieces o' paper ;
　' One's i' my pocket, and one *here*—stuck inside o' my hand.'
'*Paper*, you innocent thing !' cried Robert, 'why, this is a bank-note !
　' This is a Five-Pound Note ; ay, and yon t'other's a *Ten* !
' Which did her ladyship give ?   And which one come fro' the Colonel ?'
　' *This* be the Colonel's,' she said : 'this, with a scribble o' *Ten*.

' How could I know what they was ?   I never ha' seen nothing like 'em :
   ' Never, i' my born days, seed such a paper as yon ! '—
Robert beheld her and smiled : her ignorance never displeased him ;
   But Mrs. Jellifer's laugh burst like a shell in the air.   2200
Eh, what a story was this, when time and occasion should offer !
   Eh, what a choice of a wife Robert, poor Robert, had made !
Still (for she knew very well that my Lady exacted obedience)
   She, for the sake of the swain, suffer'd our Dolly to stay ;
Nay, condescended at length to be grimly and grandly benignant :
   Asking of this and of that : hoping she wasn't afeard.
So that the stillroom-maid, coming up to *Pugs' Parlour* * for orders,
   Bore to her fellows downstairs news of a mighty event :
How that Deceitful Old Thing has company out o' the common—
   Not the head keeper, of course ; *he* was a natural guest—   2210
But the low wench from the farm, as they say he is going to marry :
   She is up there, if you please ! *sits*, where her betters must stand !
Ay, and she's going to have tea—tea and toast, and the company teapot—
   Just like a real lady's-maid, 'long of Old Jelly herself.
Ay, and I listen'd, and heard—I, Emma, the maid of the stillroom—
   Heard 'em go on about gifts, what has been give to the girl :
Money, and dresses, and that : and how wonderful good o' the Colonel,
   Giving as much as he did ; more nor my Lady herself !—
Bah ! If the homely affairs, the hard honest toil, of a kitchen
   Bear to be treated in song (yes, and, believe me, they do ;   2220
Being a part of our life, of the drama of human existence,
   Neither unfitted to breed womanly natures and pure)
Yet in their baser forms—and all things droop into baseness,
   Idly forsaking the work Nature has set them to do—
They have a look so depraved, so deeply and darkly disgusting,
   Even the tolerant Muse shudders, and passes them by.

* The name given by kitchenmaids and suchlike creatures to a housekeeper's or lady's-maid's
m, wherein they may not adventure to appear.

Not that these vices are worse than the scandal and spite of the parlour :
    Nay, when exhibited thus, wholly repulsively bare,
They to intelligent eyes represent but the sins of our own class,
    Seen as they are indeed, stript of each graceful disguise.   2230

Leave we them, then : for at least they have nothing to do with our Dolly ;
    She, though the lowest of all, envied not others who climb :
She, too obscure to be base, too simple of heart to be vulgar,
    Rested content with her lot ; finding her happiness there :
Finding all happiness there, as they two walk'd home in the moonlight,
    Robert and Dolly, alone under the favouring skies ;
Rapt in that silent hour of intense ineffable union
    Granted, just once in a life, if they deserve it, to all.
For, in the hush of the night, in the stillness of woodland and valley,
    Robert and Dorothy heard voices as clear as their own :   2240
Voices, too rare for the ear, but quick as its life to the spirit,
    Telling of infinite hope, uttermost love and desire ;
Promising joys that would come when the sweet church bells should have ended—
    Joys in a work-a-day world never, ah, never fulfill'd.

YET, there was joy sincere, there was genuine hearty emotion,
    Then, when the sweet church bells rang for our Dorothy's day :
When she came back from the church, with Miss Mary herself for her bridesmaid,
    Back to dear White Rose Farm, back to the hearts of her friends ;
When, at the last, she went on her husband's arm, in the evening,
    Up to her own new home under the skirts of the wood :   2250
Up to the keeper's house, that lonely and lovable cottage
    Set in a pure green thwaite close to the sheltering trees ;

Listening at even and morn to the musical sigh of the pinewoods ;
　Gazing o'er garden and garth down to the light of the stream.
Yes, there was joy—and surprise : for, lo ! at the wedding dinner,
　Set by the sugar'd cake Missis had bought for her Maid,
Lay such a letter—a real large envelope, brought by the postman :
　Written ' at White Rose Farm ;' written ' to Dorothy George.'
Dorothy George ?　Who is that ?　' Why, Dolly, lass, has thou forgotten
　' All 'at has happen'd to-day, all 'at we've promised in church ?　　　2260
' Didn't I promise to love and honour and worship thee always ?
　' Didn't thou take me for thine—all of me, even my name ? '—
Dorothy blush'd at the thought : at last then, this day of her wedding,
　She had an honest name ; ay, and a name that was *his* !
His name, come to be hers : her own, to last her a lifetime :
　Telling inquisitive folks *whom* she belong'd to, and *how.*
Ah, what a wonderful thing—what an honour, she thought, what a blessing !
　Why, did you ever, she thought, see such a thing as this here—
Me, sitting up so smart, with *him*, at the top o' the table ;
　Me, 'at was servant till now, standing, and waiting on all.　　　2270
But, for her letter, she said, ' I canna tell what to do with it :
　' It's the uncommonest job ever I had i' my life ! '
' Open it, lass ! ' they cried ; and with awkward innocent fingers
　She for the very first time open'd a letter, and read—
Rather, attempted to read : for the lawyer's jargon within it
　Bore, to her unwarp'd mind, hardly a meaning at all ;
So that she handed it soon to the lord of her heart, to her bridegroom,
　Whispering, ' *You* 'll maybe read ; *I* canna skill it, indeed ! '—

' Colonel St. Quentin ' it said (for we render it now into English)—
　' Colonel St Quentin has heard much about Dorothy George ;　　　2280
' How she has lived all her life in one respectable service :
　' How she is known as a girl quiet, hardworking, and good.

'And he has seen for himself that this character does not belie her :

  'Modest, he sees her to be ; capable, comely, and kind.

'Also, he knows Robert George for an able and excellent keeper ;

  'One who'—but here Mr. George skipp'd a few words as he read—

'One who richly deserves, being an honest man and a true one,

  'Thus to obtain his desire ; thus to be blest in a wife.   2290

'Therefore, to mark his sense of this happy and suitable marriage,

  'Colonel St. Quentin himself wishes to portion the bride :

'Giving her money to spend, and something to bring to her husband ;

  'So that she shall not arrive quite like a penniless maid.

'And he has placed in the Funds, in her husband's name—for he trusts him—'

  'Ay, he may well !' cried George ; 'sure, every penny's her own—

'But, what is this, that he says ? My goodness, why, it's a fortune !

  'Neighbours, you mustn't suppose _I've_ had a hand in all this—

'But he's a gentleman born, is the Colonel, if ever there was one !

  'Well, it's _Five Hundred Pounds_—all for my Dolly and me !'—   2300

Fancy the joy and surprise, the wonder, and also the envy,

  Roused by such tidings as these, fresh from the Colonel himself !

Fancy the change that was wrought, _instanter_, in Dorothy's favour—

  She, unimpeachably now proved a most suitable match !

Nay, it was Robert, it seem'd, not Dolly, who ought to be envied :

  Robert, obtaining with her all that a marriage should give.

Fancy, the folk, how they stared ! From the Master and Missis and Mary

  Down to old Carter John, down to that Billy the boy ;

Down to that pert little Poll ; who declared, to have luck like our Dolly's,

  She were content to have hands almost as dreadful as hers.   2310

Fancy poor Dolly herself, her turmoil of pride and confusion,

  Hearing such praise of herself utter'd in presence of all ;

Thinking, while those fine words were read by the lips of her darling,

  'Why has the Colonel wrote ? What should he know about _me_ ? '

As for the money, it seem'd an enormous incredible marvel :

  Only she thought with herself, 'Maybe, it's better for _him_ ;

'When I get old, too old to work and do for my husband,

'Pr'aps it'll serve for us both ; yes, it'll keep us, and more ! '

But, when the guests were gone, when even the bride had departed—

For she had stay'd to the end ; habit, affection, and choice

Making her eager to work ; and, as if she were still of the household,

Wrought as a servant still ; clearing the tables away, 2320

Bustling at this and at that, with her sleeves tuck'd up to her elbows ;

Teaching the new-found maid how to inherit her place :

And, when all this was done, she, Dorothy, tearful and tender,

Clung to her mistress still, clung to the house that she loved ;

Thanking them oft and again for the wedding bonnet, the dinner ;

Grateful, but wholly untaught how to express it in words :

Saying, she hoped they would still let her help in the washing and cleaning ;

Hoped they would send for her still, still let her work on the farm :

And at the last, with a kiss—yes, a *kiss*—from Missis and Mary,

And from her Master, a warm grasp of his fatherly hand ; 2330

She, with a smile and a blush, clinging fast to the arm of her Robert,

Went to her own new home, up by the skirts of the wood ;

Where, among sheltering trees, soft breezes blow of an evening ;

Where, over garden and garth, shimmers the light of the stream.

THEN, when the guests were gone, and Robert and Dolly departed,

And in the kitchen remain'd Missis and Mary alone ;

Then, with triumphant air, did the good wife say to her daughter,

'Didn't I tell it thee, lass ? Didn't I say it was *him* ?

' Dost not remember them gloves our Dorothy left at the Squire's,

' What Mrs. Jellifer brought home in her pocket, to-day ? 2340

'Well—I had known all along, Dolly had 'em upstairs in her attic :
  ' They was her father's gloves ; all 'at was left her of *him.*
' Ay, for I kept 'em for her ; never thinking, nor never expecting,
  ' He would turn up like this : him, and his Griffin, an' all !
' He had a Griffin, you know, on the seal what he put to his letters :
  ' Well—when I look'd i' them gloves, there was the Griffin, inside !
' Nay, there it was, sure enough ; I could tell it, as easy as ever :
  'And there was writing as well ; C., and a bonny St. Q. !
' What does that stand for, eh ?   Why, of course it stands for the Colonel :
  ' Didn't they call him *Charles*?   Isn't *St. Quentin* his name ?
' Look—for I've gotten 'em here ; I kept 'em, to show to the master :
  ' *This* 'll persuade him, I lay ; *this* 'll speak out if it's true !
' Well—as our parson says, its wonderful, even in this world,
  ' How many things comes out, folks 'd be glad to keep in :
' Think of a man such as him, a Parliament man and a Colonel,
  ' Having a daughter like *her*, bred to the work of a farm !
' Lass, it's a senseless thing, and clean contrary to Natur :
  ' Ay, an' he's rued it, an' all ; you may be certain o' that.
' Still, he's behaved this day like a gentleman born, has the Colonel :
  ' Giving such money as yon : making her happy for life.
' Money ?   What more could he do, for a wench 'at is only a servant ?
  ' Married above her, indeed !   What's a head-keeper to *him* ?
' No !   An' I'll never no more have the heart to say nothing again him ;
  ' Never !   I reckon he's done all such a father could do.
'And I ha' settled in mind, an' thou must promise me, Mary,
  ' Never to tell o' this tale ; not to let Dorothy know.
' Why, she was fit to burst out, if ever one spoke of her father ;
  ' Maybe, she'd think it a sin, touching his money at all.
' Telling 'ud do her no good : a father she couldn't get on with ;
  ' Him and his gentlefolks' ways, what are they good for, to *her* ?
' Ay, and our Robert as well, *he* wouldn't be glad of it, neither :
  ' Keeper, and him with a wife known to be kin to the Squire !

No—we must leave 'em alone wi' their luck ; and well they deserve it :
  ' Dolly was daughter, almost—more nor a servant—to me ;
' Almost a sister to thee : and *one* thing I'll tell thee, Miss Mary ;
  ' We shall be lucky indeed, finding her equal again ! '

VENIT summa dies, et ineluctabilis hora !
  Yes—we have come to the end, come to the Colonel, at last.
Where has he gone ? Why, of course he has gone to the South, for the winter :
  When shall we see him again ? Why, with the Session, of course.   2380
Session, or rather, indeed, that happier period, the Season ;
  Not for St. Stephen's alone lives the society man :
When the asparagus comes ; when salmon is fresh at the table ;
  When from their premature beds strawberries enter, and cream ;
When there are people in town, and one rides in the park as a duty,
  Then too shall you, the Advanced, welcome your Colonel again.
Ah, he will come with his *Bill to Regulate Female Employment* !
  Ready for action again : true to each popular cry :
Ready once more to preside, with eloquence sweet and perennial,
  Over his feminine friends, champions of Freedom and Light :   2390
He, with his crotchety men and his masculine angular women,
  Fighting—and who is their foe ? Only Dame Nature herself.—
' See,' cry the feminine men and the gaunt irrepressible women,
  ' See, how a woman goes bound, fetter'd, and crippled, through life !
' Robb'd, by the envy of man, of all share in his active employments :
  ' Left to her piteous career—sewing, or teaching, or shame ! '

G

Granted, O eloquent men, O gaunt irrepressible ladies !
 Granted : and what would you have ?   What do you wish us to do ?—
' Do ?   Why, admit her, of course, to a share in those active employments ;
 ' Give her the option at least, whether she'll have it or no ;
' Give her a voice and a vote : if we *must* have laws to be bound by,
 ' Let her at any rate feel *she* had a hand in them all.'—
Oh, my adorable friends, my eager irascible females,
 Have you such faith in your sex ?   Do you, ah, *do* you desire
They should be free to work ; no longer confounded with children
 (' Women and Children,' you know—*that* is the Parliament phrase);
Using what labour they like, as strength and as Nature allows it,
 Freely and fairly, like men : shut out from nothing, save crime ?
Then I demand your applause for my tale, just happily ended :
 How you must love and admire hardworking Dorothy George !
' *Love and admire*?' cry they, with screams of angry derision—
 ' Love and admire a wench, following horses at plough !
' Love and admire hard hands, all rugged and horny with labour—
 ' Thick red muscular arms—shoulders as broad as a man's !
' What !   Do you seriously think that *these* are the rights of us women ?
 ' Booby ! and can you suppose *this* is the goal we desire ?
' No, we have loftier views : if we offer to share your employments,
 ' 'Tis but the higher we want—such as are pretty and nice :
' Such as bring fortune and fame, and honour and early preferment :
 ' Such as our Colonel enjoys—such as would never suit *you* !
As for those coarse-grain'd slaves, those ignorant arduous creatures
 ' Brutal with open-air work, toiling like Dorothy George,
They shall be stopp'd—that's all !   Their work isn't fit for a woman :
 ' Man, the sole drudge of the earth, *man* shall perform it, alone.'—

Ah then, my logical friends, most courteous and candid of ladies,
 Now we can quite understand—*now* we conceive you, at last !

Now it is clear that your Bill to Regulate Female Employment
  ('*Regulate*'—excellent word ! same as *abolish*, I see)
Means to abolish at least one half of Woman's employments :
  Means to diminish her rights : means to imprison her will.   2430
This, we perceive, is the use you would make of your votes, if you had them :
  Voting restriction of rights sacred and strong as your own !

Thus, if a maiden there be (thank God, there are many in England)
  Muscular, hearty, and strong ; fitted for out o' door work ;
Eager to do it, and apt for farm work, field work, pit work ;
  She must abandon it all : she must be govern'd by *you* !
True, she has strength and skill, and liking and taste, for her labour :
  True, that the labour itself has not a touch of reproach :
Yet she must yield, and withdraw to the ways and the work of a weakling ;
  Wasting her strength indoors, losing her cherish'd employ.   2440
Facts ? What are facts, if you please, when theories choose to ignore them ?
  When, in the place of good-sense, sentiment models the law ?

Fools ! (for I answer you now in your own sweet method and manner)—
  Fools ! If she chooses to work, *who* has the right to say No ?
Ay, if she choose to fulfil the rudest masculine labour—
  Vain of her prowess, perhaps ; glad of a livelier world—
If she be earning her bread as a soldier, a sailor, a navvy ;
  Brawny and swink'd at the forge, black in the deeps of the mine ;
Or (as myself have known a comely and virtuous woman)
  Bred to the ostler's trade, breeches and gaiters and all :   2450
Ay, if she even do *that* ; who are you, who am I, to forbid her ?
  She a grown woman, who says, ' *This* is the work I enjoy :'
She a grown woman, and free ; a wife with consent of her husband ;
  Widow, or damsel adult, needing no sanction at all ?

What? Does it lie in *your* mouths to prohibit a woman from working?
    You, who are always at hand, telling all women to work?
You, who so warmly resent the lofty pretensions of manhood,
    Would you bring down on your sex laws that are fashion'd by *men?*
Parliament?   Marry come up!   The State is the Parliament's master,
    Surely ; and who are the State?   Women, or only the men?
Why, all the men in the land, with the 'women and children' to back them,
    Have not the right to forbid labour that is not a crime !

No, my political friend, my Colonel accepted of women,
    Leading your boisterous nymphs, graceful Lyæus, around ;
Whether in Parliament pent, or careering at large on a platform,
    You and your virulent nymphs have not converted us yet !
No—there may certainly be, as the prophet says, in our England,
    So many millions of folk, chiefly and hopelessly fools ;
But we can most of us see, we commonplace practical English,
    That which is true holds good whether one likes it or not.
If it be true and confest that a woman (remembering always
    Nature has laid upon *her* tasks of her own to endure)—
If it be true and confest that a woman has courage to labour ;
    If she has sinews and strength, if she has heart for the work,
And if the labour itself be such as Humanity bears with,
    Then she may do it, of course ; whether we like it, or not.

Ah, but I think he is changed, our stately yet affable Colonel,
    Since he came back to the club, since he saw Dorothy George.
Finding a daughter like her—obscure, unacknowledged, a servant ;
    Whom an aristocrat sire never could venture to own ;
Finding, however, that she, hardhanded, clumsy with labour,
    Still had a beautiful face, still had a womanly heart,

Still, through her hardworking life (or, haply, because of it, even?)
 Kept herself healthy and pure, grew to be stalwart and strong,
Kept herself tender and true, till her warm unsullied affection   .
 Flow'd, at the touch of his love, all to her Robert alone :
Seeing all this for himself, with his own eyes, not with another's,
 Surely, I think, he is changed ; come to a happier mind.
Surely, ashamed of his *Bill to Regulate Female Employment,*
 He will have sense to avow that which his senses have seen :   2490
Leaving to *doctrinaire* dames the impertinent crazy endeavour
 Thus to give women restraints none would impose upon men.
So that, deliver'd at last (for *doctrinaire* follies, unaided
 Save by the breath of conceit, sullenly whimper and die),
Still may the peasant girls and the sturdy matrons of England,
 Bred to an open-air life such as their elders enjoy'd,
Duly become, like them, the mothers of masculine workers,
 Fit to maintain, to enlarge, England's historic renown :
So that each lustier lass, who breathes the sweet air of the country—
 Or if, unhappy, she dwell deep in the horrible town—   2500
Still may have part with her men, in the work of the land that she lives in ;
 Still may be seen, if she will, following horses at plough.   2502

FINIS.